WHISPERING CEDARS

By
Debra Hughey

www.scuppernongpress.com

Whispering Cedars
Debra Hughey

©2022 Debra Hughey

First Printing

The Scuppernong Press
PO Box 1724
Wake Forest, NC 27588
www.scuppernongpress.com

Cover and book design by Frank B. Powell, III

All rights reserved. Printed in the United States of America.

No part of this book may be reproduced or transmitted in any form or by any means, electronic or mechanical, including photocopying, recording, or by any information and storage and retrieval system, without written permission from the editor and/or publisher.

International Standard Book Number ISBN 978-1-942806-43-1

Library of Congress Control Number: 2022907455

Table of Contents

Foreword		iii
Chapter 1	1740, St. Marks Parish, South Carolina Colony	1
Chapter 2	Land Belongs to Red Man	5
Chapter 3	Let Us Wait	9
Chapter 4	Boy Baby	13
Chapter 5	Warning and Willow	17
Chapter 6	Fingers of Orange	19
Chapter 7	The Arrow	23
Chapter 8	Injun	27
Chapter 9	Tell Ma and Pa	31
Chapter 10	Ma's Fit	35
Chapter 11	Bear Stalker, Pa and Ma	39
Chapter 12	The Wedding	41
Chapter 13	The War Party	43
Chapter 14	The Attack	47
Chapter 15	The Funeral	49
Chapter 16	It's Yer Pa	53
Chapter 17	Swaying Cedars	55
Chapter 18	"Baby"	57
Chapter 19	Panther John	61
Chapter 20	"Joyce"	65
Chapter 21	"Willow"	69
Chapter 22	1747	75
Chapter 23	Spirit at Rest	79
Chapter 24	1754, New Friends	83
Chapter 25	Absalom, Choice and Mary	87

Chapter 26	Truly Blessed	91
Chapter 27	"Yes, John"	93
Chapter 28	Husband and Wife	97
Chapter 29	Panther's Visit	101
Chapter 30	A Different Ceremony	105
Chapter 31	John Was a Good Man	109
Chapter 32	Cowpens	113
Chapter 33	Alabama Bound	115
Chapter 34	To Find the Tallapoosa	119
Chapter 35	Startling Experience	125
Chapter 36	The Best Thing to Do	129
Chapter 37	Sweet, Sad Song of Dixie	131
Chapter 38	Floating in the Wind	133
Chapter 39	A Dam	135
Epilogue		139
Acknowledgments		141
Photos		143

Foreword
Spring 2022

The world is a strange place. On one side a crazed, power-hungry dictator kills hundreds of people to take their country. On the other side, Chinese scientist created such havoc in their laboratory that people were forced to wear mask and avoid crowds, practically shutting this country down for two long years. Millions of people world-wide succumbed to this virus known as Covid-19. Is there any wonder people are tired and stressed?

My answer to this situation is this book. Get a cup of coffee or a glass of iced tea and settle down in a nice comfortable place and get ready to relax and forget about the problems of today's world. Come with me now to a different place and time. Meet the Griffin family and learn of the trials, tribulations and oh yes, the happiness of these people who lived long ago. Journey with them throughout time for nearly two-hundred years. I promise your stress will be gone. Are you ready? Then let's go.

— Debra Hughey

1740
St. Marks Parish
South Carolina Colony

Chapter 1
Cloud That Fell from the Sky

The young man paused, wiping the sweat from his face. Hearing the rumble of distant thunder, he shaded his eyes from the brilliant sun and looked toward the horizon. He had not noticed until now the heavy bank of clouds that had formed from out of nowhere. The clouds were dark and ominous and surely predicted upcoming storms. Shaking his head, John Griffin picked up the old hoe he had dropped and quickly resumed the job of removing the weeds from around the knee-high corn. He knew he would need to hurry. He could smell the rain in the air and the clouds were moving closer. For two days it had been much too hot for May and he had noticed this morning that the two cows and old mule had acted strangely. When lightning zig zagged across the now darkening sky, John realized he had waited too late to make it back to the cabin. He would have to wait out the storm, somewhere.

Suddenly, the sky became dark as night and balls of ice began to fall. Trees were swaying violently from side to side and the crash of thunder and lightning were continuous. Instinctively, John dove for a slight dip in between the corn row and covered his head with a branch from and oak tree that landed beside him. He watched in terror as the cloud fell from the sky, moving across the little patch of corn and beans into the forest. He could smell the fresh scent of trees as they snapped from the top and some ended with their roots high in the air. Torrents of cold hard rain began to fall and the little dip that had been John's refuge quickly filled with water. Jumping from the ground, he ran blindly in the direction of the little cabin he shared with his family. His Pa and brother Joseph had left early that morning to help build a new cabin for his oldest brother, Joshua. He was suddenly filled with fear. He could not see through the heavy rain. Was the cabin still there? His Ma and three older sisters who had come to visit, had no place to go and would be horrified.

John felt relief when the little clearing came into view. Large limbs from the surrounding trees were scattered over the area around the cabin and the lean-to where he and his brother slept in the warm weather was crushed, but the little cabin was still intact.

"Ma! Ma!" he called out frantically. "Ma, are you alright?"

The unhued wooden door was flung open and a white-faced woman followed by three young women rushed out, fear still obvious on their faces. "John, oh John, yes we are alright. I was afraid for you," Joyce Griffin said as tears ran down her cheeks. "John, you have been hurt," she continued as she looked at the drenched clothing and hair of her son. "There is blood running down your arms. Come inside and let me look at you."

John looked at his arms and saw the stream of blood running from each. "Ma, I am alright. It is only a scratch. A limb from a tree must have hit me. I did not notice," he replied.

"John, you should have come home before the storm hit. You could have been hurt badly or even killed," Joyce admonished as she wiped the blood from his arms. She reached up on the shelf that lined the cabin wall for John's only other pair of pants and home-spun shirt. "Here, put on these dry clothes," she said as she pulled the curtain that hung on a rope, the only privacy the little cabin provided.

"Ma, the storm hit so suddenly. I did see the heavy clouds, but I figured I could finish what I was doing. When I looked up again, it was right on me," John paused. "Ma, I ain't never seen such before. A big cloud dropped out of the sky and ice balls as big as apples dropped all around and I remember hearing a roaring sound. Ma, I was afraid I was going to die right then and there," John said, realizing the close call that he had. "Ma, I think the corn was all broke over and the beans too. What will we eat, Ma?" John asked with concern. "And Ma, what about Pa and Joe? I hope they are safe."

"Hush now, your Pa knows how to get out of the way of storms. I'm sure he is fine," Joyce Griffin said, "when the rain stops, we will go out and see what the damage is and how big ah mess we got to clean up," she continued, hoping that John could not hear in her voice the fear she felt. She was very concerned about her husband and oldest son.

The hard rain stopped just as quickly as it had begun, and the bright rays of the sun peaked from behind the vanishing clouds. John opened the door and he, his mother and sisters stepped out on to the tiny porch. Joyce gasped as she looked out at the little open space around her home. Every inch of ground was covered with large limbs and small trees. The shed-like barn that Joseph had finished just last week was nowhere to be seen and neither were the cows or the old mule.

"Oh! Oh!", Joyce began as tears formed in her eyes. Pausing and taking a deep breath to calm herself she continued, "Thank you Lord for saving us and our home. Dear Lord, please let my Joseph and the boys be safe." As if on cue, loud voices were heard coming from the tree-filled path.

Looking up at the sound of voices, she knew so well, Joyce ran to meet her husband and son, nearly tripping over the debris. "Oh, Joseph, Joe, oh thank you Lord," she cried out with tears running down her face.

"It's alright honey, don't you cry," Joseph Griffin said, reaching out for his wife. "We are alright." Looking around to see if his son and daughters were all accounted for, he continued, "I am relieved to see that all of you are safe as well. Thank goodness our cabin is still standing. Many are not and I am afraid that some lives were lost down in the settlement near the river. Don't know for sure how many, but it was bad, real bad."

Turning to look at his property, Joseph took the hand of his wife and walked back to the cabin. "Joyce, if you could fix us up a little something to eat and after I rest a little bit, me and the boys need to go to the settlement. There is work to do down there and, and," he paused, "graves to be dug. You and the girls stay here and clean up what you can. We will be back before nightfall."

Chapter 2
Land Belong to Red Man

Two years had passed since the day of the storm. The little settlement down by the river had been hard hit. Most of the cabins had been picked up by the violent wind, scattering the meager belongings of those who lived in them for miles. Five people, two old men, two women and a child had perished, devastating the tiny community. The child, a little girl who had just celebrated her fourth birthday, had been sorely missed. People still talked about the child's sweet smile and sparkling blue eyes. The victims of the storm had been placed side-by-side, the child in the middle, underneath an old cedar tree. It was said by those who attended the service that after a tearful group had sang *Alas! And Did My Savior Bleed*, and the old preacher had said Amen, the old cedar tree began to sway in the breeze and seemed to whisper the word Caroline. The little girl's name had been Caroline.

The Griffin family had survived the blunt of the storm, only suffering minor damage to the small log cabin. The new barn that Joseph and his sons were so proud of had to be rebuilt, but that was alright too, as the cows and mule had been found two days later underneath the sprawling limbs of a huge oak tree. There was no money to replace the livestock. And the family, like other folks living along the little river, had to make do the best they could. The corn crop had been totally destroyed too, but the beans and squash had been protected by the fallen corn stalks. The vegetables along with the rabbits and squirrels that abounded in uncleared areas of the woods, that had not been in of the path of the storm, provided enough food to their family as well as the others. They were after all well accustomed to hard, difficult and sorrowful times.

The brothers and sisters of John now had married and were starting families of their own. They all had built small cabins chinked with plaster and lived either close by or in the little settlement that the storm had nearly destroyed. John saw the difficulty his pa had as he worked his little plot of land and did the daily chores. He also had heard that more folks were coming from the old country and were planning to settle in the area. He realized his pa needed him now and he had also noticed that there seemed to be more signs of injun activity. They had been quite for several years now and had not caused any problems for the groups of white families who were building their cabins closer and closer to the land of the red people. They were mostly the Cherokee and a few other smaller tribes. While they had been quiet, the encroaching presence of the white man had been watched, closely.

Joseph and John were out in the uncleared area before the sun rose. The land grant Joseph was entitled to extended for about another hundred yards and would certainly allow for the planting of more crops. Smiling slyly the night before, Joseph had said that he might even plant some different things, maybe some rice that grew in the low country or even some tobacco, like what they planted on the other side of the hills. Both would be valuable.

The men had put in a good morning of work, first chopping up the dead trees that covered the new land and then using the crosscut saw to take down the live green trees.

"John, my boy, think we will save this oak and that hickory over there. Make some mighty fine wood for something," Joseph laughed. "Like a cabin for you and a wife," he laughed again. "You are planning on taking a wife ain't ya?"

"Pa, you trying to run me off or some'in?" John asked, laughing with his father. "I ain't even got a girlfriend."

"Times ah comin' Johnny, times ah comin'. Let's head on back to the cabin. Yer ma will be fixing us up some vitals. Do think I'll have to rest a spell afore we come back to the field. I be mighty tired," Joseph said, rubbing his back.

Hearing a rustle in the leaves, both men stopped and looked in the direction of the noise. John moved to get his old musket he had propped against a tree. Never know when a mean old rattler might show his ugly head. Expecting to see a snake or maybe a rabbit, Joseph and John were startled to see two Indian men starring back at them. Their dark features in a deep scowl. They showed no fear in being discovered. Both held bows and the youngest placed his hand on the knife at his beaded belt.

Regaining his composure, Joseph yelled out, "you there, what ya want? You need to go away from here."

Without moving a muscle, the older of the two looked at Joseph, his black eyes flashing in anger. "Land belong to the Congaree. You go. We come back with new sun." The two Congaree then turned and vanished into the forest.

Chapter 3
Let Us Wait

Joseph sucked in his breath and let it out again in relief. "Boy, think we got trouble. We need to get on down to the settlement and let the folks there and along the way know about our visitors."

"Pa," John began, his voice unsteady. "Pa, you think they'll come back tomorrow like they said or are they just trying to scare us?"

"Don't know for sure, but we don't need to take any chances. Quick as we eat us something, we'll be on our way," Joseph answered. "I hate this, the Injuns been mighty peaceful for a long while."

The sun was at its midpoint in the sky when Joseph and John started their way down the path that led to the settlements. Joseph had assured Joyce that they would return before dark and not to worry but maybe she should stay close to the cabin, just in case the Congaree came back.

They stopped first at the home of John's sister. "Sarah, Sarah," Joseph called out. "Where are you?"

"Pa, what ya doing here this time of the day? Is Ma alright?" The attractive young woman answered as she tucked a strand of damp hair back under her bonnet with one hand and rubbed her large stomach with the other.

"Yes, yes, your Ma is just fine," Joseph said, smiling at his daughter. "Girl, looks like we gonna have a new baby real soon." Changing his tone and demeanor quickly, he continued, "Sarah, where is Denne?" I need to talk with him, right away."

"Why, he's down by the crick. What's the matter Pa?" Sarah asked, puzzled at her father's behavior.

"Just need to talk with him. John, you stay here and see if your sister needs for you to help her in anyway. I'll be back in a few minutes and we'll continue on down the path."

"John, Pa looked a little flushed and he sure is acting strange. Is he feel'n well?" Sarah asked as she reached for a basket that hung from the side of the cabin.

"Here, let me get that for you. Looks like you might bust if you reach too high. Sarah, I should let Denne tell you, but guess I might as well go ahead," John paused.

"Yes, go ahead. What is wrong?" Sarah asked concerned.

"Me and Pa had visitors from over the hills this morning," John answered. "Two Indians told us we had to leave, that our land was theirs and that they will be back tomorrow."

"Oh dear," Sarah sighed softly, rubbing her stomach again. "John, what will we do?"

"Don't know for sure, but I speck we need to be ready. We're going on down to the settlement now to let folks know, "John answered. "Now don't worry. We'll put a plan together. Try and hold off on having that baby for a day or two if you can." He smiled and touched his sister tenderly on her cheek.

"John be careful," Sarah said.

"I will. Pa's been hinting that its time for me to find a wife," John replied, laughing.

Sarah nodded and smiled at her brother just as her father and husband came around the corner of the cabin.

"Sarah, I'm going with your Pa and John. Plans must be made right now. I want you to stay inside until I return," Denne said, quickly kissing his wife. "Ring the dinner bell if you need help. Someone will come quickly. All the folks know that's the alarm for trouble."

The three men stopped at all the little cabins on the path and soon were at the settlement with the men and older boys following close behind. After telling of the alarming news, Joseph stood and held up his hands to quiet the men who were all talking at once.

"Listen to me please," Joseph shouted. "We need to prepare for a possible attack. Let us talk one at a time and make our plans."

"Let's go kill'em before they kill us," One of the men yelled out."

"That's right, we can't let them kill us first," Another one agreed.

"I ain't scared of no redskin," A rough-looking young man screamed out, waving his old musket high over his head.

Joseph finally settled the group down and cooler heads prevailed. It was decided that everyone should be extremely cautious and be on guard. Joseph suggested that no one travel far from his cabin and never alone. Perhaps this was only a scare tactic. The Injuns had not caused any problems yet and he thought it best for white folks not to start anything now. "Let us watch and wait and see if any action will be required."

Chapter 4
Boy Baby

A week had passed and there had been no sign of any Indians. The settlement folks and the others who lived along the path had not let their guard down but continued to go about their daily routine. Fields had to be plowed and food hunted for and preserved.

Sarah bent to pick up the pot of hot water from the fire and instantly felt the stab of pain in her lower back. "Oh!" She screamed out, remembering her ma had told her that was how labor pains began. "Oh, my goodness. Oh, my goodness, what am I going to do?" She cried out again, bending double in pain. She knew that Denne was helping her pa and John clear the new land and that her ma had gone to the settlement to sit with a sick friend. It would do no good to ring the bell. No one would hear.

Sarah screamed again, this time in fear instead of pain. Two Indian men, a woman and a younger woman walked up the path into the clearing. Sarah continued to scream, backing away and holding her stomach.

"Not hurt," one of the men said, turning to look at the woman, while saying something in his language that Sarah could not understand. The woman nodded and smiled at the frightened woman.

"Baby come," she said softly. "Soon." The Indian woman moved closer to Sarah and held out her hand. "Come." Sarah stepped back again as yet another pain gripped her. "Help," the Indian woman repeated and motioned toward the cabin.

Sarah knew then that the pretty Indian woman with sparkling jet-black eyes meant her no harm but instead was going to help deliver her baby. She smiled at the woman as she sank to the ground in another wave of pain that consumed her whole body.

The woman spoke to the man who was obviously her husband, again in the tongue of their people, and he immediately scooped Sarah up and went inside the cabin. He placed her on the bed, the dry corn husk rustling under her weight. The Indian woman then spoke to the young woman with her, who then brought the pot of hot water inside.

The man joined the other man outside and both sat down on the log bench and pulled their pipes from the beaded pouch on their belts. This would take some time, both men had this wait before.

Sarah now was crying uncontrollably, and she wanted her ma. She looked into the eyes of the Indian woman and knew this woman was now her ma. In between the excruciating pains, the now calm young woman pointed to the older Indian woman and whispered, "Name, your name?"

"Wind, me Windsong Woman," she pointed to the young woman who was wiping Sarah's face with a warm cloth, "name Willow." She pointed to Sarah.

"My name is Sarah," she said as the pain came again.

"Sa-ra," Windsong Woman smiled. "Baby come. Sa-ra, good." The Indian woman felt Sarah's stomach and smiled again. "Sa-ra push."

Seeming like an endless time to her, Sarah pushed and cried and pushed some more. Windsong Woman continued to hold her hand while Willow wiped her face. After and hour had passed, the final big pain hit, and Sarah thought she would surely die without ever seeing her baby. She screamed loudly.

"Sa-ra push hard!" Windsong Woman said softly.

Denne and John were walking up the path and heard the chilling scream. "Sarah!" Denne cried out and broke into a run. Both men were surprised, frightened and then angry when they saw two Indian men sitting on the log bench outside the cabin.

The Indians were expecting them and the response they would have. Their bows and knives where lying at their feet. They stood and the husband of Windsong Woman greeted the men in a friendly voice. "No hurt, help baby."

Suddenly from inside the cabin, the loud cry of a baby filled the air. Looking from the Indians to the cabin, Denne rushed toward the closed door. The other Indian man stepped in front of the door. "Man wait," he said. Denne frowned, then realized he did need to wait when he heard the voice of Windsong Woman softly talking to Sarah.

Windsong Woman asked Willow to go find bear grass and liquid for Sarah to drink. The birth had been hard, and she would need the drink to help her heal. She then went to the door and motioned for Denne to come inside. Sarah looked exhausted but happy as Windsong Woman placed the baby, that had been wrapped in a blanket into her arms. "Boy baby," she said as she stepped to the other side of the cabin.

Chapter 5
The Warning and Willow

Windsong Woman allowed Denne and Sarah time to enjoy the miracle of birth until Willow had the bear grass concoction prepared. She then took the baby from Sarah and in a kind voice, ordered Denne to leave. She smiled at him and indicated that Sarah should drink the liquid and rest.

Denne joined John and the Indian men outside. John smiled at Denne, "Congratulations. I assume all is well with Sarah and the baby."

"Yes John, I have a son," Denne answered, smiling broadly. "And Sarah is doing just fine." Looking at the Indian men, he added, "Thanks to the Indian woman." Becoming serious he continued, "I do need to know who you are and what you were doing sitting on my bench? I do have to admit that the timing was good."

Standing, the older of the two extended his hand in white man fashion. "I Bear Stalker. This man friend, name Wolf. We are Cherokee. We come from Cherokee land to warn white man of danger from other tribes. We on path and hear woman cry in pain. My woman name, Windsong Woman, help. White woman have hard time. May be not live if we not come."

"Thank you, thank you," Denne said softly. "I will always consider you and your woman my friends. Please tell me more about the danger."

"The Congaree people live on this side of hills. Say white man come close to village. Say come burn cabins. Want Cherokee to help. Cherokee no help. Come tell white man," the tall Cherokee man answered.

Looking in awe at the Cherokee man, John asked, "How is it that you speak English so good?"

Bear Stalker smiled, "Traitor live close village. Spend time with him. Learn white man talk."

As the men were talking, Windsong Woman and Willow

quietly slipped out of the cabin. John looked at Willow and his eyes locked with hers for a brief moment. The young woman quickly looked down. Windsong Woman smiled at Denne saying softly, "Wife and baby good. You take care?"

Resisting the urge to hug the Indian woman, Denne answered, "Yes, and her mother will return soon. She will take good care of them."

Windsong Woman nodded. "You need eat. Fix stew before go?" She asked, looking at Bear Stalker.

"Yes, need food. Talk more with white man. Make stew."

Moving back into the little cabin, Windsong Woman quickly found the items she would need for the stew. Willow paused and looked back at John before joining her mother. John could not take his eyes from her. She was the most beautiful woman he had ever seen. Willow shyly smiled. John's heart began to beat so loudly, he hoped no one else could hear.

Bear Stalker told of the pending danger and that the settlement people needed to be on the alert. The Congaree people were few, but fierce warriors and enjoyed takin' scalps. After the stew was finished, Bear Stalker looked at the sky and said that it was time for them to go. The sun would no longer shine before they reached the land of the Cherokee.

Denne and Bear Stalker warmly clasped hands and Denne again thanked Windsong Woman, this time giving into the urge and hugged her. "Thank you again for helping us. Please come to see the baby."

"We come when danger gone. Not come down path now. No safe," Bear Stalker said, placing his bow on his shoulder.

John looked at Willow and both smiled. He knew he would see her again and he hoped it would be soon.

Chapter 6
Fingers of Orange

Four weeks had passed, and the settlement folks had continued to be vigilant and nervous. They had planted rows of corn and squash, always keeping a watchful eye along the shadow of the tree line. No one had seen any Congaree or any other injuns, yet.

Some of the women had decided it would be nice to have a little get together with some good food and maybe old Joe could bring his fiddle. They had all agreed that it would be good to relax and enjoy themselves for a time. So, it had been arranged on Saturday next long 'bout noon time. All the settlement folks would meet in the big open meadow where they planned to build the Methodist Church. Some of the men had volunteered to roast turkey and venison, while the women were delighted to bake fresh bread and make sweets from honey and wild berries. Old man Smith had whispered to the men that he had a jug or two of the "good stuff" that he would be happy to share. The folks were all excited about the upcoming get together.

Saturday dawned clear and warm and promised to be a beautiful day. The morning was spent in last minute preparations and finally, in little groups of three or four, the settlement folks began the short walk to the meadow. Some of the men had hastily constructed tables made of pine for the food to be served. The children, screaming with joy, soon began their play and the women gathered to gossip and swap new recipes for making stew. The men sat under a big cedar tree, puffing their pipes and talking of the threat of an injun uprising. They agreed it best for someone to be on guard at all times, just in case. They also were thrilled to see old man Smith coming down the path with his jugs of the "good stuff."

The Griffin family had come, happy to show off the new baby boy. Denne and Sarah beamed with pride and John told over and over of how they had heard Sarah scream and finding two Cherokee sitting on the bench outside the cabin. Joseph and Joyce had happily watched their family and were glad to visit with their other children who lived in the settlement.

The merriment continued, and the abundant food was consumed, with even some left over. The sun was beginning its descent in the western sky, and old man Smith had shared the contents of his jugs. Old Joe was tuning up his fiddle, and the younger folks were pairing off to dance. The dancing and singing continued well after bright moonlight filled the night. Everyone was happy and having a joyful time. Then, as one of the young men swung his sweetheart round and round, he saw a red glow on the horizon.

"Look," he yelled, pointing and nearly dropping the young lady.

"That's in the direction of my cabin." Another, named Ben yelled out, as he broke into a run.

The others grabbed their muskets and followed close behind the young man. "Some of us need to stay and guard the cabins here," Joseph yelled out, gathering the women and children around him. "Come, hurry," he ordered, pointing them toward the center cabin of the settlement, picking up buckets as they ran. He knew they had to be prepared.

The bright glow grew larger, and fingers of orange lit the skyline. It was evident that the home of someone was going up in flames. When the men reached the clearing, they heard loud whoops and saw several Indian men slipping into the woods. The owner of the nearly destroyed cabin attempted to follow but quickly retreated as he felt the stab of pain from the arrow that pierced his arm. The other had immediately formed a bucket brigade, passing buckets of water from the little creek to douse the fire.

"It's gone Ben," one of the men yelled out. "Sure sorry. Better come, let me get that arrow out of your arm. The injuns done gone. We can't catch 'em."

"How am I gonna tell Bette. She was so proud of our little cabin," Ben answered wincing in pain as the black arrow slick with blood was pulled from his arm. "She wanted to fill it with young'uns," he paused, "and one's on the way."

"Ben," the other man said, "we will build you another one," he smiled. "A bigger one to hold all the young'uns."

"Yeah," still another said, "we'll get started jest as soon as we get this mess cleaned up and we'll fill it with supplies fer you. Them injuns think they can scare us. We ain't going no place else."

"Thank you," Ben said. "Thank you all so much."

The Congaree braves stood just outside of sight of the still glowing embers of the cabin, their painted faces menacing in the flickering light. "We will return," one said with a final whoop and turned toward the path that led back to the hills.

Chapter 7
The Arrow

The settlement folks were unnerved and downright scared when the injuns had ventured on to the land they claimed as their own. Why, they weren't bothering them injuns, what right do they have to come anyway? No one had been hurt too bad and the cabin would be rebuilt real soon, but the very idea! Well, they had said, the folks would jest be ready for'em next time.

The next time would come sooner than the folks had expected. The foray by the Congaree had been to check things out and to see how many people lived in the settlement and surrounding area. On the next full moon, they planned to return and there would be more than five braves this time. Their neighbors, the Catawba had eagerly agreed to make the trip down the valley with the Congaree.

The settlement folks had all met together the day after Ben's cabin had been torched. John Griffin had told them that he and Denne's new Cherokee friends had come to warn them of an upcoming attack. It was suggested that maybe John and one of the other Griffin brothers could make the trip over the hills to Cherokee land and ask for help.

"I don't like that idea at all," Joseph Griffin chimed in. "It's much too dangerous. They would have to go right through them Congarees to get there."

"No, they can go the long way," someone else said quickly. "Might take a little longer but it would be worth it."

After more discussion, it was agreed that John and his brother Joshua would go, and they would leave immediately. Joseph hugged his sons and told them to be real careful and not take any chances. "Best not let your Ma know. She wouldn't like it a'tall. One of the women here will fix you up some vitals. I think you can get to Cherokee land by night fall," Joseph said, suddenly looking like the old man that he was. "Please use caution my boys."

The Griffin brothers had taken the path further down the valley and had seen no sign of the injuns and were within a few miles of the hills and Cherokee land. They had been watchful and made as little noise as possible, the Congaree could be anywhere. By midafternoon, having not stopped to rest or eat, the brothers decided they would do so before making the last leg of the trip. Leaning against a big oak tree, John saw movement in the bushes and instantly felt the arrow move deep into his leg. Joshua rolled over just in time, escaping the same fate. To their amazement arrows flew through the air coming from the other side of the bushes. The sound of loud whoops filled the air as several Cherokee men ran toward the bushes, scattering the Congaree warriors who ran in the direction of their village.

"Bear Stalker," John cried out. "Bear Stalker, it's me, John Griffin."

"I know John Griffin," the Cherokee man said smiling. "We have been on your trail long time. You get too close to Congaree. You come to Cherokee?"

"Yes, we were sent by the settlement folks. Bear Stalker, we need your help. They attacked us, doing only slight damage this time. We know they will return," John said breathlessly.

"They will," Bear Stalker answered, looking at John's blood-soaked britches. "You have bad wound. Get you to village." He motioned for Joshua to help him get John to his feet and together they continued on to the Cherokee village. The two braves who were with Bear Stalker kept a close watch to make certain that they were not being followed by the Congaree.

Travel was slow but the village was reached just as the first stars began to shine in the night sky. The dogs announced their arrival and the village people rushed to greet them. Bear Stalker called out for Windsong Woman to quickly come. Windsong Woman followed by Willow, immediately recognized the young man.

"John Griffin," she exclaimed. "What you do?"

Looking over her shoulder, John saw Willow and smiled in spite of the terrible pain he was feeling. "Congaree found me. I will be alright."

"You will, when arrow out of leg," Windsong Woman answered him, touching his face. "You hot. Need bear grass. Make cool." Looking at Willow, she continued, "Go get bear grass. Make drink for John. Then bring sofkee and grapes. He need eat, later."

John was taken inside the cabin of Windsong Woman, which was similar but different from his own. He then was helped to lie down on the couch-like bed that lined the wall. The Cherokee woman bent closely to John to cut his britches from around the arrow wound. Ma ain't gonna like this he thought as he gazed at her face. He saw warmth and compassion in her eyes and could not help thinking that this woman, like her daughter was beautiful.

"Deep in leg," Windsong Woman said, as John winched in pain. She gently wiped the area with a damp cloth made from hemp grass. "John brave?" She asked seriously. "John need firewater to kill pain?"

"No, I can take the pain," John answered, hoping that he could. He had never had an arrow cut from his leg before.

Windsong Woman smiled at him as Willow entered the cabin carrying a clay cup half full of the bear grass drink. John was embarrassed for her to see so much of his leg, but relaxed when she stood by his side lifting his head as he drank some of the liquid from the cup, her deep brown eyes shining with concern.

Windsong Woman smiled again. "John ready? Pain big. Willow hold hand. John still," Windsong Woman whispered as she picked up the knife, the tip red from being placed in the fire.

John could not keep his eyes open and fell into a deep sleep. When he awoke, the cabin was dark except for the glimmer of fire coming from the pit in the center of the room. He moved his leg and nearly screamed out in pain. He realized he was not alone. A tiny figure was sitting on the couch across from him.

"John not move. John still," a small, sweet voice softly said.

He had not heard her speak before but knew instantly it was Willow.

"Willow," John called out.

"Yes, John. Me Willow. You need be still," She ordered. "Arrow deep. You rest. Feel better."

John nodded and drifted back into a fitful sleep. He did not know his body was hot with fever. Willow knew and she constantly wiped his face with the cool damp cloth.

Darkness turn to the gray of dawn and Willow kept her vigilant watch over John. Windsong Woman and Bear Stalker had slept in a nearby cabin, with Windsong Woman checking on John several times during the night. She had not planned on the fever but was confident that he would recover. Willow would see to that.

John woke to see the fingers of sunlight streaking through the open door of the cabin. Where was he, he thought, then remembered the arrow and Willow. Suddenly, she was at his side, touching his face and smiling. "John no hot. John better. John eat now," Willow said happily as she went to get her mother and the sofkee that was filled with sweet, wild grapes.

Windsong Woman decided it best for John to stay with the Cherokee until his leg had completely healed, that would be many suns she was sure. Bear Stalker had said he would send several braves back to the settlement with John's brother. They could at least be watchful and help the folks prepare for the attack that was sure to come.

Chapter 8
Injun

John's leg had been slow to heal. Windsong Woman had watched as the red streak down his leg became brighter and the heat returned to his body. She had prepared the bear grass poultice for the wound and the liquid for him to drink. Willow would leave his side for only short periods of time. Both had prayed to the One Above that he would recover.

After five suns had passed and Windsong Woman had gone deep into the forest for stronger medicine the red streak began to fade, and John's strength returned. Willow still stayed with him when she could. She was then reminded that she had other responsibilities. Windsong Woman could see that her daughter had eyes for this white man called John.

John realized this was not supposed to happen, that his feelings were considered inappropriate. He was a white man; she was a Cherokee maiden. Ma would be furious. That did not change the fact that he was madly in love with Willow and she him.

John was also concerned about his family and what was going on at home. There had been no report of any attack on the valley settlements, but even the Cherokee were upset regarding the increasing numbers of white people coming nearer the Cherokee homeland.

Bear Stalker and John had talked the day before regarding the need for John to return home and also of the white people. The men had high regard and trust for each other. Neither wanted any problem to arise between them because of the situation.

"John," Bear Stalker said as he puffed on his pipe. "Windsong tell me you well. Me take home when ready. Talk with white people. Avoid trouble, maybe." He paused, before continuing. "John, me know you have looked at Willow. What you do?"

John was totally caught off guard by the question. He had

no idea that anyone knew about his feelings for the beautiful Cherokee maiden. "Bear Stalker, I, I do not know," he stammered. "I do not know if she shares my feelings."

"Face of daughter turn red when look at you. Eyes shine. Me think she do," Bear Stalker answered.

"What can we do," John asked softly. "I don't know what my Pa and Ma will say when I tell them that I love a Injun maiden. Where would we live?"

Bear Stalker stood, a stern look covering his face. "You not hurt her." If John think Willow is a Injun, John need go home alone. Find ugly pale face white woman for wife!" The Cherokee man stalked off in anger.

John swallowed the lump that formed in his throat and he felt as if he had been punched in the stomach. "What have I done," he said out loud to himself. "I want only Willow for my wife."

Neither man had known that Willow had been sitting on the other side of the cabin and that she had overheard the conversation between her father and John. Tears ran down her beautiful face as she walked around the cabin to face John.

"Come with me," she said, taking his hand. "We talk."

Willow and John slowly walked down the path that led to the creek. Her small hand was warm inside of his and he could smell the sweet scent of her jet-black hair. They sat down on a large rock that bordered the rushing stream. Willow looked at him, tears still glistening in her dark eyes.

"John love Willow?" She whispered, touching his face.

He nodded, taking both of her hands. "Yes," he answered. "Does Willow love John? Will Willow take a white man for a husband?"

"Willow love John. John think Willow Injun? Not be wife." She stood, taking her hands from his, her eyes twinkling in humor. "Willow Cherokee, not Injun."

John smiled at her, enjoying the game he knew she was playing. "Willow," he said. "You are the most beautiful woman either Cherokee, Injun or white that I have ever seen in all my borned days." He laughed as he pulled her into his arms and for the first time, he kissed her. Doing what he had wanted to do since the day their eyes had first met.

Chapter 9
Tell Pa and Ma

John apologized to both Willow and Bear Stalker for referring to Willow as an Injun. He had promised never to call any Cherokee that again. He was after all going to be part of their family. Bear Stalker said that John should go home to see his family and tell them of his plans to take Willow as his wife. He had smiled and said he knew they would be happy. Bear Stalker said that he and two braves would escort John home in two suns. He had said that he should check on the activities of the Congaree and Catawba.

John had tenderly kissed Willow the night before the planned trip back down the valley to his home. He and Bear Stalker had decided to be well on their way before brother sun showed on the eastern horizon. He had held her close, savoring her touch. When he released her, he again saw tears in her dark eyes. "Why do you cry Willow," he had asked concerned. "I will return in a few suns and then we can be married in the way of the Cherokee."

"Your Pa and Ma," she had answered, referring to them as John had. "Them not be happy. Not allow you come back."

"Willow, I am a grown man. I make my own decisions," he said remembering that he had thought the same thing himself. He hoped Ma wouldn't throw one of her fits. He knew she had hopes of getting him married off to one of the settlement girls, one with blonde hair and blue eyes. He kissed Willow once again and softly whispered in her ear that he loved her, and she would soon be his wife. Bear Stalker and John, along with the braves traveled fast and saw no sign of activity from the Congaree. The valley seems peaceful and quiet. The underlying plans were well concealed. Continuing on they did meet a family in an old rickety wagon headed north up the valley. The man and woman looked tired and worn out and the three small children had dirt-smired faces, their eyes large and showing fear.

"Whoa! Whoa! The man yelled out to the two hollow-sided

mules, "stop there." Relief covered his face when he saw John with the Indian men.

"Where you head'n," John asked as the man eyed Bear Stalker.

"Don't know," he answered. "Jest got to get away from them Injuns. They showed up at my cabin and made me leave. Said they'd kill all of us if we didn't."

"Are them Injuns gonna kill us," the oldest little boy asked as he wiped his nose on his shirt sleeve.

"No," John answered, "these are Cherokee, not Injuns. They mean you no harm."

"Injuns ah Injuns," the man said, still looking at Bear Stalker.

"No, they are not," John said strongly. "If you keep going the way you are going, you will find some Injuns and they will kill you. Best turn around and go back to one of the valley settlements. There is safety in numbers, and they'll share food with you."

"How'd I know that when I turned back you and them Injuns, ah, I mean Cherokee want jest shoot me in the back and take my family," the man asked with more strength than he felt.

"Man do as told," Bear Stalker said sternly. "Not ask questions. Go."

"Think we'll jest keep going the way we's going," the man answered defiantly. "The way I figure it, we's gonna die anyway. Like I said, ah Injun is ah Injun. I would appreciate it if'n you jest move out of my way."

"Mister, you gonna be sorry," John said surprised as he and Bear Stalker moved so that the man and his family could pass. Both men shook their heads as the old wagon creaked up the path in the direction of the Congaree, who were waiting patiently.

The sun was high in the sky when John and Bear Stalker reached the outskirts of the settlement. Men and women were busy with their chores and the children were at play. Two or three men did seem to be on watch but did not see John and the

Cherokee. John noticed that Bear Stalker and the braves had stopped. He turned and asked, "Bear Stalker, are you coming with me? I would like for you to meet my Pa and Ma."

"No, not go," Bear Stalker answered. "You tell make Willow wife. Come back for you new moon. You bring Pa and Ma, if them come."

John nodded as the two men clasped arms in Indian fashion. "We can make the trip. You do not need to come back for us."

"Not safe. Bear Stalker come. Be ready to be husband to Willow. You take good care," Bear Stalker said, softly as he vanished into the forest.

"How do they do that?" John said out loud. The settlement dogs had noticed John's arrival and announced it to the settlement folks who rushed out to greet him.

Chapter 10
Ma's Fit

The family members of John who lived in the settlement were happy to see him and that he had healed from the injury he had received from the Injuns. He did not tell them of his plans to marry a Cherokee maiden his Pa and Ma should be the first to know. After he had rested and eaten a big bowl of venison stew, he left for the cabin of his parents. He would stop to visit with Sarah and Denne on the way, and he was anxious to see the new baby.

Denne was in the clearing near the cabin chopping on the trunk of an old oak tree when he saw John on the path. "John, John," he exclaimed. "My friend it is good to see you, and that you are well!"

"Yes, Denne, I have healed from the arrow wound and it is good to see you too," John answered. "Is my sister well and how is the new baby?"

"Come and see for yourself," Denne said happily as he grabbed John's hand. "Sarah, Sarah," he yelled. "Look who's back."

"John, Oh John," Sarah screamed as she ran from the cabin, clutching the baby close. "Look at little Denne John. He is such a beautiful baby."

"He is that," John said, hugging his older sister. The two had shared a special bond, different from their other siblings. "And did you name him after me too?"

"I did and I am so happy to see you. You look so happy. Do you want some food," Sarah asked breathlessly? "Them Injuns must 'a taken good care of you."

"Had food down in the settlement," John said smiling. "And yes, the Cherokee did take care of me, very good in fact, but please don't call 'em Injuns."

"Why John, what's happened to you? You look like the cat that just caught a mouse," Denne chimed in. Is there something you need to tell us?" Denne smiled remembering the look that had passed between the Cherokee girl and John.

"Well, yes there is," John answered smiling even more broadly. "Was planning to tell Ma and Pa first but I can't hold it in any longer. Me and Willow are going to be married just after the next new moon."

"Willow, the girl that helped her Ma when I gave birth to little Denne," Sarah asked?

"That pretty little Injun, ah, I mean Cherokee," Denne added. "She's a looker alright, but I didn't spec you'd take it this far. John are you sure you want'a do this?"

Before John could answer Sarah said seriously, "John, you know Ma will throw a fit. She was just talking the other day 'bout how you should court that Sally Johnson. That she'd make you a fine wife and her Pa's got a little money too."

"Sarah, listen to me," John said as they walked to the cabin to get the baby out of the hot sun. "I love Willow. Have since the first time I laid eyes on her. She loves me too. Ma will just have to have a fit."

"Where will you live? You gonna be an Injun or are you gonna try to make a white woman out of her?" Denne asked with scorn in his voice.

"That ain't been decided yet. I had hoped the two of you would be more understanding than this." John paused, "did you not say to Bear Stalker that you and he would be friends forever? I, I want you to come to our marriage celebration."

"Of course, we'll come," Sarah said with tears forming in her eyes. "We'll work this out. Ma said that me and little Denne might not have lived if the Injun, ah Cherokee woman had not been there."

"Denne smiled sheepishly," ah, I did say that didn't I. Guess I was not thinking about us being family. Sarah is right, we will work this out. Never been to an Injun," laughing he corrected himself again, "I mean Cherokee celebration before. John, just so I can get this straight, what is the difference between and Injun and a Cherokee?" Denne asked.

Smiling at his brother-in-law, John answered, "don't really

know, but Bear Stalker said the Cherokee were not Injuns. They think more of themselves than that. They call themselves "The Principle People," and I do know that they are more civilized and act better that those Congarees. Reckon I'll find out more as time goes along. Now I need for both of you to come with me to tell Ma and Pa about my soon to be new family."

"Wouldn't miss this for nothing," Sarah said, "but I gott'a feed little Denne John first. Denne, you and John wait outside. This won't take long."

In a short time, Sarah reappeared with the baby placed in a cane basket, loosely covered with a woven blanket to keep the bright rays of sun from burning him. "We're ready now," Sarah said happily, "this should be interesting."

"Yes, very interesting," Denne added as they started down the path that led to the cabin of Joseph and Joyce.

John's stomach filled with butterflies, and his mouth became dry as they approached the cabin, the place he called home. His Pa and Ma were inside, Ma sitting at the churn and Pa working a piece of leather into a new bridle bit for the old mule.

"John, son you are home!" Joyce cried out, nearly turning the churn over as she jumped up to hug him.

"My son, it is good to see you safe and sound once again," Joseph said as he too hugged John.

"Ma, Pa it is good to see you too," John said happily.

"Come sit down, tell us all that has happened to you," Joyce said as she took the baby from his basket cradle. "Sarah, how are you and Denne John today? Denne, I hope you haven't been out in this heat too long."

John sat down and told them of the experience he had been through and how kind the Cherokee had been to him.

"That is good son," Joseph said. "The Cherokee are good Injuns."

John, Sarah and Denne burst out in laughter. "What's funny," Joseph asked in confusion.

"Pa, the Cherokee are not Injuns," John answered, realizing this was the opening he needed.

"What are they then," John's father asked?

"The Cherokee will soon be my people, my family. Willow will soon become my wife," John finished as he looked at his Pa and Ma.

Joseph and Joyce were stunned, silently looking at their son. Finally, Joseph spoke. "Son, you cannot be serious."

"I am Pa," John answered. "I love Willow and she loves me too."

Joyce began to cry at the words she heard her son say. "John, please do not do this to us," she pleaded.

"Pa, Ma, it was not my intention to hurt you. You have always taught me to be true to myself and follow my heart," John said softly. "My heart led me to a Cherokee maiden. I have done the necessary things that their way commands. Her family will accept me as their son. Please accept her as your daughter."

Joyce was the first to speak after another long period of silence. "My son, part of me wants to scream and shout and even take my cane and whack you on the head," she laughed, tears still shinning in her sad eyes. "But what good will that do?"

"Your Ma's right, and you are right. You have followed your heart," Joseph added. "We too will accept her, and we will call her Cherokee and not Injun."

"Thank you," John said, hugging Joseph and Joyce. "Will you come to the marriage celebration?"

"Don't know about that. May have to think on it for a while," Joseph said with humor showing on his face.

John was happy that Ma had not thrown a fit and whacked him on the head with her cane. He knew his Pa and Ma would be a part of the upcoming celebration for him and Willow.

Chapter 11
Bear Stalker, Pa & Ma

Two days later, before the sun rose, John was awakened by a strange bird call, one he had never heard before. Hearing the call, a second time he jumped from his bed, grabbed his old musket and headed out the door, thinking the Congaree Injuns had returned. To his surprise, Bear Stalker was waiting for him near the edge of the trees.

"Bear Stalker!" John exclaimed. "I was afraid it was them Congaree Injuns again. Why are you here now? I was not expecting you yet."

"Time for you come Cherokee town. Get ready, be husband for Willow," Bear Stalker answered. "Glad you know bird call signal from me. Make good Cherokee."

"John," Joseph called out. "What's all that racket out there?"

John smiled at Bear Stalker and asked him before he answered his Pa, "Come meet my Pa?"

Bear Stalker nodded and stepped from behind the trees.

"Lord ah mercy, an Injun," Joseph yelled out.

"Pa, Pa," John exclaimed! "Settle down, this is Willow's father, Bear Stalker."

Joseph eyed the Cherokee, looking at him from head to toe, obviously not trusting him. Then as their eyes met, Joseph smiled. "I am Joseph Griffin. I believe your wife and daughter helped my daughter in the birthing of my new grandson. I thank you for that."

Bear Stalker returned the smile. "My wife helped bring many baby into world. First time white. Good."

"Pa, Bear Stalker said it is time for me to return to the Cherokee and prepare for the celebration. I will return for you, Ma, Sarah and Denne the day before," John said.

Bear Stalker held up his hand and shook his head. "My people," he paused, "my people fear so many whites in our town. Want one come with John. Sorry for, for," he paused, searching for the right word in English.

"It is alright Bear Stalker," Joseph began. "My family are a little uncomfortable going to a, ah Cherokee town. So, this solves our problem too."

John looked relieved that the problem was so easily resolved. "I think it best if Denne comes with me."

"Denne, good," Bear Stalker answered. "Leave when sun shows face."

"Not before I fix up some breakfast," Joyce said from the cabin doorway, an iron frying pan in her hand," I am John's Ma," she said, looking at Bear Stalker.

Not knowing how to acknowledge the woman with twinkling eyes that showed of humor, Bear Stalker just smiled at her and said, "break-fast good."

"Never had ah Cherokee at my table before. First time for everything. Guess I'll have your daughter eat with me many times," Joyce smiled. It was obvious that she had taken a liking to Bear Stalker.

"Thank you, Ma," John said. "Me and Bear Stalker will go get Denne and Sarah while you get breakfast together. He will need to prepare to go."

The family enjoyed the time with Bear Stalker and were more at ease with him. They had been amused as he tried to fit himself into a chair and slide to the table.

John hugged his Ma and Sarah just before he, Denne and Bear Stalker headed up the path toward the hills. "Ma, when I come back, I will be a married man. I know you and Pa have been waiting for that for a long while."

Joyce nodded and smiled but thought to herself, "but not to an Injun, I mean a Cherokee."

Bear Stalker turned to Sarah and Joseph and said, "good meet you. Food good. Watch for Congaree Injuns. They come soon."

Chapter 12
The Wedding

John was told what to expect and what was expected of him. In the time he had spent healing from his arrow wound, he had made many friends among the Cherokee, and they were excited about the upcoming celebration. Willow looked more beautiful to him than before, and when he kissed her on his return, he whispered that she soon would be his.

On the night before the marriage ceremony, John was told that he would eat and spend time with the shaman on one side of town while Willow would be on the other side with her friends. They would have no contact with each other.

The sky was filled with bright sunshine the following morning, and the entire town buzzed with excitement as they filed to the town council house for the ceremony. As their custom, the oldest men sat on the high seats on one side while the oldest women sat on the other. The next seats were filled by the next oldest and continued until the council house was full. As a guest, Denne had been invited to sit near the bottom with the younger Cherokee men. In awe he watched with much curiosity and anticipation of what would happen next. He and John were the only white people in the entire town of Cherokee, and he admitted to himself that he was also more than a little nervous, in fact, he was downright scared. What in the world was John thinking? These Cherokee people and the way they lived were very different from what he was accustomed.

A loud rap on a drum announced the beginning of the ceremony. A priest escorted John to one end of the open space in the center of the council house. Then a different priest escorted Willow, beautifully dressed in a white deer skin dress to the other end. Since the mother of John was not present, the sister of Windsong Woman presented him with the leg of deer and a blanket. Windsong Woman then gave Willow an ear of corn and a blanket. John and Willow then walked to the center near the sacred fire and exchanged the deer and corn. Looking at each other, John and Willow joined their blankets together, thus pledging their love and support for each other. They were then considered by the Cherokee, man and wife. John took Willow's hand, and together they walked to a cabin on the outskirts of town that belonged to a clan member.

The following day, all the people assembled at the square ground for another feast and much dancing. The marriage celebration between John Griffin and Willow had been enjoyed and was the first in the town between a white man and a Cherokee maiden.

Chapter 13
The War Party

John and Willow were blissfully happy with John becoming more familiar with the Cherokee. He knew it would take time for him to totally understand them and their way of life. He also knew he would never agree with some of their practices. For all they said about themselves, they were after all different from white folks. After a month had passed, John decided it was time to take Willow home to meet his Ma and Pa. He hoped that he could convince her to accept the white man's way of life and they could make their home there.

He had told Bear Stalker that they could make the trip back to the settlement alone, there was no need in him going, unless he and Windsong Woman would like to visit with Pa and Ma. Denne had made the trip back to the settlement the day after the wedding ceremony. Windsong Woman had said she would enjoy meeting John's Pa and Ma. Bear Stalker had told her about the gentle old man and lively woman that had sparkling eyes. Windsong Woman had prepared bread and roasted deer for them to eat along the way. She had also dyed strips of river cane and had woven a brightly colored basket as a gift for Ma.

John and his new family enjoyed the journey down to the settlement. He and Bear Stalker had become close friends and he had grown to love Wind Song Woman. He knew few white women who had such a caring manner and was always ready to help anyone in need.

The August sky was crystal clear and a wide-open view of the horizon could be seen for miles. Just as the family began the descent down into the valley, Bear Stalker pointed to the circle of smoke that rose from the tree line. "Fire"! He said.

"Oh no, that's in the direction of the settlement," John shouted as he began to walk faster.

"John, I fear Congaree and Catawba on raid," Bear Stalker answered. "Nothing we do to stop. We need help."

Continuing on as quickly as possible and getting closer to

the outlying cabins, they could smell the scent of smoke. John was almost beside himself with fear for his Ma and Pa and this brothers and sisters. And what about Sarah and Denne? Willow and Wind Song Woman suddenly stopped and began to chant. John turned and looked at them in surprise and was about to tell them to hurry.

Bear Stalker touched John's arm, "they pray to One Who Lives Above for safety of your family. The ancients of our people prayed this way."

In a short time, the prayer chants were finished, and they resumed, walking at a fast pace. The women barely able to keep up with John and Bear Stalker. Soon they were in the valley and suddenly heard the sounds of close by war whoops. Bear Stalker placed his finger to his lips, indicating silence and pulled Wind Song Woman and Willow from the path, with John following close behind. Fortunately, a trail from deer that led to a ravine, deeply covered with vines, concealed them from the war party. John had his musket ready and Bear Stalker notched an arrow on to his bow string.

The group of about twenty warriors passed by, totally unaware of the family hidden in the ravine. John had been horrified at the sight of a scalp of red hair dangling from the belt of one of the warriors. He knew several men with red hair.

Once the group of warriors had moved on down the path, the family continued on their way, with John practically running ahead of them. When the outskirts of the valley settlement came into view, John stopped short, shocked at what he saw. The smoldering cabin was a total loss and the roof of the little shed caved in as he watched. The cows and mules nowhere to be seen.

Catching a movement out of the corner of his eye, John gasped as a hysterical young woman looked at him, her hair a tangled mess, dirt mixed with tears streaked her face and her homespun shirt was torn. She screamed again when she saw Bear Stalker.

Bear Stalker shook his head and backed up, indicating that

he was not going to hurt her. Wind Song Woman instinctively moved toward woman, speaking softly and holding out her arms. The young woman looked at her and slowly fell into the arms of the Cherokee woman.

John and Bear Stalker then saw the bodies of a man and woman, lying in a heap behind the burning shed. Expecting the worse they were relieved to see movement and heard a low moan. Rushing to them, John gently pulled the woman away from the man, his eyes staring vacantly back at them. Bear Stalker shook his head and closed the eyes that would never more see. The woman looked at Bear Stalker and tearfully asked, "Why?"

The strong Cherokee man gently took her hands into his and answered, "Bad Injun. I sorry."

John and Bear Stalker covered the man with limbs from a pine tree, telling the woman they would give him a proper burial when they returned. Leaving Wind Song Woman and Willow behind to comfort the old woman and her daughter, they continued to the settlement, fearing what would be found.

Chapter 14
The Attack

The smell of smoke from the smoldering cabins was still strong in the air. John and Bear Stalker stood in silence as they took in the site before them. Several of the settlement cabins were no longer there and the destruction was heartbreaking. John looked first in the direction of his older brother and sisters' cabin and to his relief they were still standing. The settlement folks were in a state of shock, with some trying to put the remaining fires out while others were seeing to their injured kin. Others, crying as they looked upon those who did not survive the attack, and there were many.

John, with Bear Stalker at his side, ran from group to group assisting in any way they could. The reaction to Bear Stalker was fear at first sight, but he was soon recognized as the father of John's wife. He was able to stop the bleeding of several men who had been injured.

John, as he bent to help a child, saw his brother coming toward him. "Joshua, Joshua," John yelled. "Thank God you are alive. Is the rest of the family alright?"

"John, I am so glad to see you!" Joshua replied. "Yes, we are all uninjured. Many of our friends are not," he said, tears streaming down his weathered face. Looking at Bear Stalker, he continued. "Why do you people do such terrible things? We did nothing to deserve this."

Expecting this response from the settlement folks, Bear Stalker sadly replied, "these not my people. These bad, bad injuns. Cherokee warn, now help."

Joshua nodded his head answering, "I know that, and I am sorry. Please help us now."

Chapter 15
The Funeral

John looked at Bear Stalker and yelled, "Help my brother! Stay by his side so that you won't be mistaken for one of the Congaree. I'm going to make sure Pa, Ma, Sarah and Denne are safe. I will return as soon as I can."

Bear Stalker nodded, "I will help."

John rushed to the path that led to the cabins of his family that were a half-mile or so away. He breathed a sigh of relief when he reached the clearing and saw the cabins still standing but seeing no one, fear clutched his heart. Where were they? He thought.

"Pa, Ma," he yelled out. "Sarah, Denne!" Seeing movement from the backside of his Pa's cabin, he watched as his Pa threw back a roughly hewn log door from out of the earth and all of his family crawled out.

"John is it safe to come out," Joseph asked breathlessly.

"Yes, Pa, the Injuns are all gone," John answered. "Where did ... what was ... how did you come from the ground," he asked in confusion?

Joseph faintly smiling answered, "sided to build us a place to hide case one of them storms or Injuns came again. Dug a hole in the ground, put some rocks inside. Believe it worked out. We were safe." Then becoming serious, he continued, "what about the settlement, your brother and sisters?"

John shook his head. "Bad Pa, it's bad. Our family is safe, but people were killed. Don't know who or how many."

"Let's go help," Joseph replied. "Ma, stay here."

"I will not!" Joyce emphatically answered as she bent to pick up her bag filled with supplies. "John, where is Willow? Is she with you?"

"Yes, Ma, she and Windsong woman stayed with a family down the path that were attacked. The man was killed. Bear Stalker is at the settlement with Joshua."

"John, go get your wife and her Ma, "Joseph demanded. "We

all do need to stay together. Windsong Woman can help yer Ma. We have got to hurry!"

John went for Willow and Windsong Woman, while Joseph and his family went in the direction of the settlement. Joseph was shocked and saddened when the little settlement came into view. He and Joyce wasted no time in rushing to help those in need, and there were many. In a short time, John and Willow, along with Windsong Woman were seen on the path and they too immediately began to give aid to the injured settlement folks.

After the injured had been attended to and plans were made for those who had lost their homes, the task of digging graves had to be done. With this completed, it was time to bury the dead.

The sun was low in the sky as the people of the now smaller valley settlement slowly and sadly walked to the hill where the victims of the spring storm had been buried. Four men, three women and two children would now be laid to rest beside them, underneath the big cedar trees. The old preacher, his face blackened by the smoke from the fire he helped put out earlier, slowly and painfully walked to the front of the tearful group. Friends and neighbors helped to support those who had suffered the greatest loss.

"My friends, my people," the preacher began as his voice broke, and tears fell from his eyes. "Today we have seen the wrath of people we do not understand. Our loss is great, and we will not see our loved ones again this side of heaven. But our God is good, and he will be with us through this terrible time. My friends, God in his great wisdom has shown us today that not all Injuns are bad. He has sent Bear Stalker, Windsong Woman and Willow from the Cherokee to help us in our day of sorrow." "Dear Lord," he began in prayer. "Bless us your children in our time of need. In the name of Jesus Christ our Savior we pray, Amen."

The sorrowful service ended with the settlement people again singing, *Alas and Did My Savior Bleed*. As the sun sank below the horizon, Windsong Woman and Willow began to sing in their soft, beautiful voices, the song of their people, one the Cherokee women had sung in their times of sorrow long ago.

Just as it had happened in the spring storm, the wind began to blow, and the old cedar trees seemed to whisper the names of those who were gone.

Chapter 16
It's Yer Pa

By the light of the brightly shinning moon John, Willow and their families slowly walked down the path to the cabin of Joseph and Joyce. Joyce insisted that Bear Stalker and Windsong Woman wait until the morning to return to their home. She stirred up ground corn, flavored with wild onions, and spooned it into the boiling bear oil, quickly preparing the meal. The two families, despite their cultural differences had formed a bond. When they finished, the men with their pipes in hand went outside to talk of the tragic events of the day and of what to expect in the future. Windsong Woman told Joyce that the ground corn with onion had been very good, but for a different taste, she should add wild grapes and berries. That was good too.

Bear Stalker and Windsong Woman had refused the offer to sleep inside the cabin, instead taking their blankets outside to the little shed. Willow had laughed when she and John crawled into his small bed, the corn husk giving way to their weight.

The following morning, John and his Cherokee family returned to the village. He promised his Ma and Pa that he and Willow would return soon for a visit. He had confided to his Pa that he hoped to convince Willow to make the settlement her new home.

The long summer filled with violence and sorrow was finally coming to an end. Only sporadic attacks had occurred mainly because the Cherokee had sent word to the Congaree of retaliation if the valley settlements continued to be harassed.

John and Willow continued to be happy, and John was adjusting to the new way of life. He still hoped that soon he and Willow would have two homes, one here with her people and one near his Pa and Ma. He had not returned to the settlement since the day the cedars had softly whispered the names of those slain by the Congaree. He sorely missed his family, and was thinking of making a trip back soon.

John and Bear Stalker had spent the early morning hunting for turkey, both for the meat and the feathers, which were used for so many things. John was rapidly becoming efficient with the bow that Bear Stalker had made for him. He was on mark bringing down his first turkey, a large tom, which would provide much meat for his Cherokee family. He knew Willow would be proud.

"John, good shot," Bear Stalker said, smiling broadly. "Now show how dress. Willow do rest."

John and Bear Stalker walked the short distance back to the village, the comradery between the two of them obvious. Hearing unusual activity, they knew something was amiss, and hurried on to the crowd that had gathered.

"Denne, Denne," John called out, seeing the husband of his sister, "is something wrong? Why are you here?" He knew, looking at Denne that something had happened at home.

"Yes, John," Denne answered softly. "I came as soon as I could," he paused, looking at John sadly. "It's your Pa. He, passed away last night."

"Pa, no!" John exclaimed as tears formed in his eyes. "What happened?"

"Think it was his heart, he just fell over while he was working in the field. We did all we could. John, your Ma's a mess. Told her we'd be back soon as I could fetch you," Denne finished, looking at Bear Stalker. "We need to go soon as we can. We want Willow and you and her Ma to come. The folks will have things ready for the burial just afore the sun goes down."

Chapter 17
Swaying Cedars

John and his family, with sorrowful hearts, quickly made the trip back to the valley settlement. They went first to his Ma's cabin where he knew the family would be.

"Denne, John!" Sarah screamed as she ran to meet her husband and brother. "So glad you are here. The preacher said it was 'bout time to go to the cemetery. Oh John," she continued as she fell into the arms of her brother. "Pa's gone and Ma ain't said a word. She just sits and stares out at nothing."

"Where is she, Sarah?" John asked, looking around for his Ma.

"Out back, on the big rock," Sarah answered.

John kissed his sister on the cheek and went outside to the back of the cabin. Joyce sat silently, looking out at the field where Joseph had been when the attack hit him.

"Ma," John said softly. "Ma, its John." She turned and looked at him. John was shocked. The happy, vibrant and strong woman he had last seen was gone. In her place was an old, wrinkled woman with pain and sorrow deep in her eyes. "Ma, it's time for us to go to the hill. Ma, it's time to lay Pa to rest." Joyce nodded and slowly stood up. John reached for her hand to steady her, and together they joined the others, and began the slow walk to the hillside cemetery.

Joseph Griffin had been well respected and considered a leader, being one of the first to settle in the valley. The same group of people apart from the many who had already made the hill their final resting place, gathered near the old cedar trees.

The old preacher, his tattered bible in his hand, stood in front of the sad people. He slowly looked at those in front of him before speaking. "Today, my brethren, we lay to rest one of the finest men I have ever known. Joseph Griffin was a friend to all and was always willing to help anyone in need." He read a few verses from his bible and led the Lord's Prayer, and they again sang *Alas and Did My Savior Bleed*. No one was surprised when the old cedars began to sway in the breeze, and many claimed to hear the name Joseph whispered softly as the wooden box was lowered into the ground.

The settlement folks all gathered with the Griffin family at Ma's cabin after the funeral of Joseph. The women had prepared various vegetables, and stews as well as cakes and pies, and everyone was invited to eat with the family. The sober event soon became almost festive as stories and the antics of Joseph were told and laughed at. John's new Cherokee family were included with Willow and Windsong Woman asked to sing a song in their beautiful language.

After the folks went to their homes, the family faced reality and the deep feeling of sadness enveloped them. Their beloved husband and Pa were gone. For safety concerns, the family decided that Joyce should live with one of her children. She had smiled and assured them that she would be fine. She could shoot Pa's old gun as well as he. They knew then that Ma was indeed going to be able to continue on with her life.

Chapter 18
"Baby"

John and Willow made the trip back and forth between the Cherokee land and the settlement. As it had turned out, they did have homes in both places, although it wasn't the way John had planned. He missed his Pa, the advice he gave him whether he had asked for it or not, the things he had taught him and most of all the twinkle in his eyes when they had their "man-to-man" talks. Joyce had been heartsick but refused to feel sorry for herself and had moved forward. Her only request was for her family to visit often. She loved Willow and enjoyed the visits from her and John and was eagerly looking forward to a new grandchild one day. That day would come soon.

The yellow and orange leaves floated through the air as John and Willow walked the path beside the rapidly moving mountain stream. They both enjoyed the time together and walked as often as they could. As John looked at Willow, he noticed a glow about her that he had not seen before. She glanced at him and smiled. "John, why look at Willow?"

"Willow, you look different today," he said as he took her hand.

She smiled again and placed John's hand on her stomach.

"Baby," she said.

"Oh, Willow!" John exclaimed as he pulled her close to him. "When?"

"In the time of ripe berries," Willow whispered.

John knew the Cherokee described seasons by using nature and that the time of ripe berries meant early summer. "Oh Willow," John joyfully spoke her name again as tears formed in his eyes. "This makes me so happy."

"Willow happy, John happy," the beautiful maiden answered.

The couple walked hand-in-hand back to the village and the cabin of Windsong Woman.

Windsong Woman was sitting outside dying strips of bark. She worked to make a new basket for John's Ma as she planned to make the trip back to the settlement when Willow and John went again.

Looking up at her daughter and John, she knew instantly that they had something to tell her.

"Willow, John," she called out. "Come, sit. Have big smile. What make happy?"

Willow placed her hand on her stomach and said again, "Baby."

Windsong Woman smiled. "Know. Baby come when berries ripe."

"How did you know," John asked?

"Tell look at Willow," she said, "Happy too.

The weeks and months of the time of the cold season quickly passed. John and Willow happily anticipated the birth of their baby. The old shaman had predicted the baby would be a boy child. Most of the women of the village agreed. John wondered how by just looking at Willow they could know. These were happy times. The Congaree had settled down and bothered no one. Word was sent to the Cherokee that a trader had come down with the fever and several of the Congaree had caught it from him and died. The chiefs and old leaders warned that the increase of white settlers coming closer to the Cherokee Nation would bring the fever to them too, and in time it would.

John, Willow and Windsong Woman had made several trips to the valley settlement during the cold time. John knew that his Ma enjoyed the company of the two women, and she too had been happy about the baby. She did wonder what the skin color of her grandchild would be. It had never occurred to her that her son would marry an Indian. She had long since stopped calling Willow and her family Injuns. They were, after all, good people, and she truly loved Willow, and knew she would love the child, whatever the color would be. She had told them not to make the trip down the valley again, that Willow's time would be soon, and she needed to be at home.

Willow had laughed when John told her what his mother had said. She explained to him that in times of long ago, the final three moons before time for birth, the mother to be would be secluded in a dwelling place far away from the village. But even then, she would also have to prayed for and be purified by a priest who could also predict the future of the child with his red and white beads.

"I could not be away from you for three months, I mean moons," John had said. He still had difficulty referring to things as the Cherokee did.

"John, I will know when my time comes and my mother will know before me," Willow had said.

Both decided it would be best if the trip to the settlement was postponed until after the baby came. And that was good.

Chapter 19
Panther-John

Two suns later, Willow picked up her blanket, and kissed John on his check, and told him she would return soon. "Willow, where are you going?" John asked. "And why are you taking your blanket?"

"John, I have to go, I have to go have baby," Willow answered, smiling.

"What, is it time? I am coming too!" John said.

"No, John not come. John wait," she said as she grimaced in pain and headed to the appointed place.

John watched her go, not knowing what he was supposed to do. He was relieved when Bear Stalker touched his arm and told him to come with him. "Cherokee women do this different," he said. "We wait together. Windsong Woman say, not take long."

Before the sun was high in the sky, Windsong Woman appeared, a bright smile on her face, "John have son," she said happily. "Baby, Willow good."

"When can I see them?" John asked with tears in his eyes.

"Soon, Willow rest now," Windsong Woman answered.

John and Bear Stalker continued to wait. Bear Stalker turned to John and asked, "How boy be raised? Cherokee or White?"

John was startled by the question but did not hesitate to answer. "He will know the way of both. The Cherokee and the White man. He will be free to choose his path." That answer seemed to satisfy Bear Stalker. He and John had only a short time to wait before he saw Windsong Woman coming toward them. She motioned for them to follow her.

To John' amazement, Willow was sitting up on the couch-like bed. She looked tired, but beautiful, and in her arms, wrapped in a blanket was his son. "Willow, oh Willow," John whispered softly. "May I see our son?"

Willow nodded and pulled the blanket from the baby's face so that John could see. From a tiny brown face, dark black eyes stared back at him. "Oh Willow, he is beautiful, just like you," John said weakly, overwhelmed with emotion.

"Yes, nose like John," she answered happily. "Willow stay here. John go eat with Windsong Woman. See on new day," Willow said as she stroked the baby's face.

The next day, John was told it was time for the blessing and naming ceremony. A priest took the baby from Willow and waved him over the fire. John jumped up alarmed at what was happening. Bear Stalker pulled him back and indicated for him to be quiet. The priest continued the process three times more, asking special blessings from the fire. John watched in amazement and fear, realizing that he still did not understand the ways of the Cherokee people. He was then told that another process would take place at the mountain creek in three suns. Now it was time to give the baby a name. Windsong Woman rose from her seat and the priest placed the baby in her arms. Willow had told John that her mother, as beloved woman, would have the honor of naming the baby. John sat in silence as he waited for Windsong Woman to announce to them what the child's name would be. She looked at the baby, who had been totally quiet during the process, and smiled.

"Son of my daughter and John have two names. He will be Panther to his Cherokee family, and he will be called John by his White family. Baby name, Panther-John."

John was elated that she chose to include his own name but was confused by the choice of Panther. "Windsong Woman," John said. "Thank you for including my name, but please tell me about Panther?"

"Night before baby come, hear Panther cry. Know strong baby come soon. Baby named Panther."

Two days later the same priest stood in the middle of the mountain stream with Panther-John. He asked the Great Creator to allow the child to have a long, happy life. Then placed his hand over the baby's mouth, and nose and dunked him seven times into the cold water. He then announced to the village by the sound of Cherokee drums the new life of Panther-John, and with a nod to his people, turned and gave Panther-John back to his mother.

Chapter 20
"Joyce"

Panther was a joy to John and Willow, and Windsong Woman adored him. He was smart and quick to learn the ways of his Cherokee people. In his fourth warm season he had shot and killed his first rabbit with the little bow Bear Stalker had made for him. He loved his grandfather and spent much time with him. Windsong Woman was quick to cook his favorite food and took him on trips into the woods in search of plants for her medicine.

Panther made the trips to the valley settlement with John and Willow to see his white family who called him Little John. He was confused by the name change but understood the best he could when they explained to him that here he was considered white. The little boy with brown skin and deep brown eyes had looked at this arm and politely answered, "me Cherokee. Not White." His dark colored hair did not defy his remarks.

Joyce, who had continued to live alone since the death of Joseph, realized her fear that her grandchild would be an Indian. After one look at him, the color of his skin did not matter. Just as his Cherokee grandmother did, she adored him and loved being with him, teaching him the ways of his White family.

"Granny Joyce," Little John said on the most recent visit. "You feel bad? Not look good."

Joyce looked at Little John intently and wondered how the child knew. No one else had commented. She did not feel well and had not for several days. She feared that something was wrong. Thinking this child was just extremely perceptive, she calmly answered, "Little John, I am just tired today. What do you think about helping me pick some wild strawberries and then we can make some sweet bread to go with them?"

"Oh, Granny Joyce!" He had exclaimed happily. "I like do that."

Joyce took the little brown hand and looked back over her shoulder at John and Willow, "we will be back later. Maybe

Willow could make some rabbit stew. Sarah, Denne and Denne John are coming over for supper." She and Little John walked hand in hand off into the large group of trees beside the cabin.

One week later, while John and Bear Stalker were hunting for deer, Denne again made the trip to the Cherokee town. His heart was heavy as it had been several years earlier. Seeing the horse Denne had proudly showed off on the most recent trip to the settlement, John knew instantly that something was wrong, and he feared it was his Ma.

"Denne," John called out, dropping the large buck he had shot. "Denne, it is Ma?"

Denne nodded, feeling like he was repeating something he had done before. "She went peacefully John. Said it was time to go be with the Lord and your Pa. John, she also said, to tell all of her children that she loved them and," Denne stopped and smiled, "John, she said to tell Little John that she was proud to have a Cherokee grandson."

John, Willow, Bear Stalker, Windsong Woman and Panther John, who nervously sat in front of Denne on his big brown horse, slowly began the routine trip back down to the valley settlement. John took Willow's hand in his and felt the comfort of her love for him while memories of his Ma flooded his thoughts. This was hard.

"John," Willow said softly. "John, she is gone to be with The Creator. John, I sorry. I love you."

John looked down at his beautiful Cherokee wife and smiled, "I know Willow, I love you too."

As they had before, the people of the little valley settlement slowly walked to the cemetery on the hill. There were many graves there now underneath the old cedar trees. The old preacher himself had passed away the year before, and a younger man who had answered the call of God, with Bible in hand slowly moved to the front of the crowd.

He stood and looked over his congregation with his eyes focused on the family of Joyce and he slowly began, "Joyce Griffin was a good woman. She loved the Lord. She loved her family and taught them to love the Lord. She will be greatly missed but she would not want you to grieve for her. Remember her and the good life she lived here on this earth. She is gone to be with her Lord and Savior." He read several verses from his Bible and prayed that her family would find comfort. They then sang the old song once again, *Alas and Did My Savior Bleed*.

Before the last words of the song were finished, as had happened before, the old cedars began to gently sway and seemed to whisper softly her name …" Joyce."

The folks were no longer alarmed by this, but no one could explain the phenomenon which was heard by all. John felt a sense of comfort by this and explained to them what he had learned from his Cherokee family. The cedar, he had said, "is widely used all across the country. The hard wood is used for building cabins, frames and mask for the Cherokee people. More importantly the boughs are used to purify. So, you see the reason cemeteries are placed near cedar trees is to purity and ward off evil spirits. This is true, both for Cherokee and Whites. The color of one's skin makes no difference." The settlement folks had nodded, many of them thinking that John was becoming Cherokee, but no one could deny what happened each time someone was buried underneath the branches of the old cedars.

John and his family had stayed the night at Joyce's cabin before returning to the Cherokee Nation. He had not been surprised when he returned and found that the cabin smelled of cedar as Windsong Woman had returned first and placed cedar boughs on the door and in the hearth. "Thank you, Windsong Woman," John said. "My Ma would have appreciated your kindness."

"Your Ma good woman. House need be purified," Windsong Woman said. "Who live here now?"

John smiled, taking Willow's hand, "I was hoping that me and Willow and Panther John could spend more time here." Seeing the disappointment in her eyes, he quickly added, "when we visit my sister and brothers."

Windsong Woman smiled. She had also quickly prepared rabbit

stew and bread using Joyce's big iron frying pan. "Pan cook good."

John looked at his sister Sarah and as if reading his thoughts, she quickly nodded and said, "Windsong Woman, I think my Ma would be honored if you take the pan home with you. I have one of my own."

Windsong Woman smiled again, "thank you Sarah, me happy to have."

The next morning John and his Cherokee family headed back over the hills to their home. John knew, other than to see Sarah and Denne, he would not often make the trip back to the settlement.

Chapter 21
"Willow"

Five-year-old Panther John continued to be a favorite in the Cherokee town. He enjoyed spending time with the grandfathers and hearing stories of the ancient ones. He was always ready to help the grandmothers with daily chores and had become a better shot with his bow than boys twice his age. John and Willow were proud of their son and hoped that in the future he would become a leader for his people whether it would be Cherokee or White.

John and his son were fishing for trout in the little mountain stream that ran near the village. Panther dropped his baited hook into the rushing water and was delighted to see the sinew line instantly become tight. "Wait," John ordered. "Let the fish pull down just a little more before you pull up."

Panther did as his father said and just at the right moment snatched the sinew line from the water. Panther smiled at the sight of the large trout that dangled from the hook. "Look, my father. I caught big fish. Grandmother Windsong cook in pan from Granny Joyce."

"Yes, Panther you are good at catching fish. Next time grandfather Bear Stalker will teach you the art of spear fishing. That may be a little more difficult," John said, proud of his son.

"I watch him. I do." Panther said with confidence. My father you white man. You kill Cherokee?"

John stared in disbelief at his son. "Panther, no. I will never kill any Cherokee. Why would you ask such a question?"

"Old man say white man come, fight, take land. Kill Cherokee," Panther seriously answered.

John shook his head. "Panther, that may happen, but I will never have nothing to do with any such action. I will fight with the Cherokee. The Cherokee are my people now."

"That good," Panther said happily. "You teach me white way. Then I know how fight white man too."

John talked with Bear Stalker later that day, and told him of the troubling words of Panther. "Panther wise for one so young. Many in village talk of white man coming. This happen, if not now, then soon. Panther understands that you are white, and he is part. Need know what feelings you have," Bear Stalker stated matter of factly.

"Bear Stalker, you know that I will never harm any Cherokee," John answered.

"Me know that. What about others of your white family? What they do," Bear Stalker asked.

John knew that his kin would never harm his Cherokee family but was not sure what would happen in the event of an attack. "Bear Stalker, I cannot answer that."

"Now you understand question of Panther," Bear Stalker smiled at John and added, "come, now go eat fish Panther catch."

Windsong Woman and Willow had fried fish and bread using the pan that had belonged to Joyce. Windsong Woman had even put wild onions in the bread like Joyce had done. Panther had smiled and quickly pulled a handful of wild berries from his pouch and asked if they could have berries with some of the bread too. John had laughed at his son, knowing that he would need to have confidence in himself when he became a man. It would be hard being both Cherokee and White.

John pulled Willow close to him as they lay on their cornhusk bed later that night. He had convinced her that this was much more comfortable than the Cherokee couch, and she had agreed. The two had combined the ways of the White and Cherokee and it seemed to work for them. Most of the village people had accepted John, but there were still some that looked at him as a white man with evil ways. There had been more talk about these men as more of them had arrived from across the big water. The Cherokee had heard from others that big towns were being built at the edge of the water. They, like Panther wondered what these white men who lived among them would do. Willow had asked him the same question.

"Willow, I have been asked this question three times today,"

John answered. "You know I will never harm your people. I love you and our son and, you are Cherokee," he gently kissed her. "And I will protect both of you from bad white men who may come."

"John protect new baby?" Willow asked sweetly.

"Willow are you with child," John asked happily. She had been in the last cold season but had to go the hut for women much too early and the baby could not survive. Willow had been slow to regain her strength and John hoped it was not too soon. "Yes, this baby come," Willow counted on her fingers the way he had shown her to do, "in five moons."

"Willow, you must take care and not work so hard this time," John said tenderly,

"Willow take care," she answered softly as she rolled over and was soon sleeping soundly.

Two weeks later, after Willow had helped skin a large buck, Panther found his mother lying in a pool of blood behind their cabin. He had run as fast as he could for Windsong Woman and then for his father. "My grandmother, my grandmother come quick. My mother is hurt. She has blood all around her. Oh, come quick!" Panther screamed, not knowing what had happened. He continued running in search of his father. When John saw the child he instantly knew something was wrong. "My mother, cabin," Panther cried out. John picked up Panther and ran in the direction of their cabin.

Windsong Woman was already there, tears streaming down her dark face. "John, help me get her to the hut for women. She not stay here."

"The baby," John asked as he put Panther down and tenderly scooped up his wife with tears forming in his own eyes.

"Yes," Windsong Woman answered. Then turning to the frightened little boy continued, "Panther, go for priest. Tell him come quick to hut for women."

Panther turned and ran in search for the old priest, and breathlessly told him his mother was hurt. The old medicine man guessing the problem with Willow, gathered the medicines and paraphernalia he would need. Entering the dark hut, the priest immediately folded back the skin flap that served as a door. He turned to John and told him to leave.

"Windsong Woman go now. Come back later," the priest said as he looked at Willow. Windsong Woman nodded, knowing that he would first use his divining beads and crystal to determine if her daughter would live or…die.

Softly beginning his chants, the old priest rolled the black and white beads between his fingers and held the crystal up to the light from the outside. Both showed the same results. He tenderly touched Willow's face. She slowly opened her eyes. "John, please tell John to come," she said weakly.

The priest nodded and went to the door and beckoned for John to come. John, with Windsong Woman following closely behind him went to the bed side of his wife. Willow looked at John and then her mother. John touched her hot face and picked up her small hand. "Willow, my darling Willow," he began, "please don't leave me."

Willow shook her head and faintly smiled, "my mother," she began, her voice so weak and soft she could barely be heard. "Let John teach Panther way of white men and," she closed her eyes again and gasping for breath, looked at John, "and John, let my father and mother show him the way of the Cherokee. He both. Let him decide how to go."

John looked tenderly at his wife, knowing her time was short. "Willow, I love you. I will allow our son to choose his way."

Smiling again, Willow squeezed John's hand and taking a final deep breath, she looked at John, "and John, I love you." Just as she closed her eyes for the final time, John saw a faint sparkle of the Willow that had stolen his heart. Now she was gone, and his heart was broken.

For five days John watched in wonder as the Cherokee rituals were performed for his wife. He then realized how different these people were from his own. He had insisted that Willow be placed near a grove of cedar trees where her grave was covered by large stones and a brightly colored blanket that Windsong Woman had made. Tears ran down John's face as he and Panther hand in hand stood by her grave. Panther had tried to be brave, saying that Cherokee men did not cry. John had told him that he was not, yet a man and white men did cry. His mother would understand and be proud. John looked up as the wind begin to gently blow and the cedars began to sway and whisper, "Willow." Windsong Woman and Bear Stalker looked at each other and then at John. Windsong Woman smiled and through her tears softly said, "Willow has walked the path the Creator has called her home."

✷ ✷ ✷ ✷ ✷ ✷ ✷ ✷

Chapter 22
1747

John wondered restlessly back and forth between the Cherokee town where he had lived and the valley settlement, he called home. He found contentment in neither place.

Panther John had gone with him on several occasions and had enjoyed visiting with his white cousins but had told his father that he was happier with Windsong Woman and Bear Stalker. John realized that his son was beginning to find his own way. He was not troubled by this, he had after all, promised Willow that Panther would be free to choose the path of his choice. John had missed Willow tremendously thinking often of the mischievous sparkle in her eyes and how proud she had been when either of them learned the different ways of the other.

That cold season John had received word that Windsong Woman and Bear Stalker had come down with the fever of the white man and walked the path. He had returned to the Cherokee town and again watched in amazement the mourning rituals. Panther John had watched wide-eyed but did not cry. He had been happy to see his father, but refused to leave with him, saying he had Cherokee family that would take care of him but that he would soon be old enough to take care of himself. The maturity of the boy amazed John. He showed strength and courage which was a true Cherokee characteristic.

When it was time for John to return to the white settlement, Panther John had clasped his father's arm as he had seen his grandfather do. John had resisted the urge to hug the child realizing that his son did not think of himself as a child. "Panther John," John said sadly. "I will come back soon to see you." Panther smiled at his father, both knew that it would be a long time, if ever before he would return to the Cherokee town.

John, still finding no peace when he returned to the valley

settlement, decided it was time for him to move on. He packed his meager belongings and after hugging his sister and shaking hands with Denne, he mounted his gray horse and headed in the direction of Charles Town. He had no idea what he was searching for but knew he could not find it here in the valley. He still dreamed of Willow, figured he would from now on.

John Griffin met Agnes in a little settlement not far from Charles Town. She was widowed, her husband had been shot in the head during an attack by rouge Catawba's. Her two little boys, ragged and hungry, had looked at John in desperation. He felt pity for them and the next thing he knew, John had a new wife and family. He did not love her and knew he never would. At first, he still dreamed of Willow, but Agnes was a good woman and he was a lonely man. She would give him two sons and a daughter. Four years later, Agnes succumbed to the fever that was raging through the settlement. Fortunately, her sister had agreed to take care of the children. John restlessly moved on again. He had planned to go back to the Cherokee town and see his son Panther John, but he could not find the courage just yet. He knew the memory of Willow would be too strong there.

Passing through a new settlement, John heard a church bell ring, and the sound of joyful singing. He stopped to listen not realizing it was Sunday. He was touched by the beautiful singing and sat down on a log bench outside the church. As the Preacher began his sermon on salvation and the love of God, tears began to stream down John's face. He had been baptized, his mother Joyce had seen to that, but he had not thought much about the Lord in the last few years. He remembered the talks he and Willow had had about his God and the God of the Cherokee. They had laughed and decided that he was one in the same, just called by a different name. Why was he still thinking about Willow, she had been gone for almost five years now? He had had another wife and children. Why did the memory of the beautiful Cherokee maiden haunt him? He did not understand.

The church service was over, and children began running out the door. The older people stopped to talk with the Preacher, telling him how much they had enjoyed his sermon. John noticed the men walking to the wagons for baskets laden with food. Must be gonna have some sort of meal, he thought as he stood to go, wiping the tears from his eyes. As he began to walk away, someone called out to him, "wait, sir, please wait."

John looked back a pleasant looking woman, maybe a few years older than himself. She was smiling at him but with a look of concern. "Sir," she said again. "I saw you sitting out here from inside and, ah noticed that you seemed to be in distress. Is there something we can help you with?"

"No mam," John answered shyly. "I was just passing by and I heard the beautiful singing and then the preacher seemed to say the words I needed to hear. I'll just be moving on now."

"Have you had anything to eat today?" The woman asked, smiling again. "We are all going to have dinner outside. We have plenty of food and you are more than welcome to join us." She paused and then continued. "And, I'm sure Preacher Daniel will talk or pray with you. He's such a good man."

Several others had gathered around, curious about the sad-looking man. "Yes, another woman, holding a baby joined in. "We have enough food for everyone."

"Yes, please stay and eat with us," yet another one added.

John suddenly realized that he was hungry, very hungry. "Thank you, I will stay and eat," he hesitated, "and if the preacher has the time, I would like to speak with him."

He followed the woman to a clearing where two log tables had been placed near several big cedar trees. Behind the trees John could see piles of rocks that indicated a small cemetery. Soon the log tables were covered with vegetables and stews and breads and of course pies. John had not had food like this since Agnes had passed away, and that had been nearly a year. He enjoyed the food immensely and the church people were all so kind to him.

When the meal was finished, Preacher Daniel had placed his hand on John's shoulder, and ask him if he needed to talk. John smiled at the preacher, who appeared to be only a few years older than he. "Yes sir, I believe I do." John told the preacher, who listened intently, about his Pa and Ma, then about Willow and his life among the Cherokee. He told him about Panther John and his desire to see him again. He then told him about Agnes and the children, how he left them with her sister and that he had wondered from place to place since then.

I can understand your sorrow, John," Preacher Daniel said.

"Sir," John began slowly, "that's not my problem."

"What is?" He asked.

"My problem is that I'm haunted by Willow. I grieve for her, not my last wife. She is on my mind, constantly. What can I do about this?" John asked, as he broke down in tears.

Preacher Daniel looked at John and smiled, "let me pray for you son." The preacher began to pray, "and dear Lord he finished, "please help this man to let go of the past, and help him to move forward, but to cherish the love and time he had with Willow."

Just as the preacher said amen, the wind began to blow, and the cedar trees began to sway. If the preacher had been a swearing man he would have sworn that he heard the name floating in the breeze. Startled, Preacher Daniel looked at the man beside him. John nodded, affirming that he too had heard. "Dear Lord," the preacher said softly. "Son, there has to be an explanation for this, but I declare, I don't know what it is." He paused, rubbing his head. "I think you should go back to the Cherokee town, find your son, go to the burial place of Willow, and pray that her soul has peace. So, that yours may as well.

Chapter 23
Spirit at Rest

John left the settlement, but not before allowing the women to wrap meat and bread in brown parchment and promising to come back for a visit after his trip to see his son. He had learned that the nice woman who had first asked him to stay was called Mary and that she too had had a hard life.

On the third day after leaving the settlement John reached the Cherokee town. The dogs met him in an unfriendly greeting, forcing him to retreat. Soon several young braves came to his rescue. It had been several years since John had visited the Cherokee people that he had called his own. How soon one forgets he thought when he did not recognize any of the braves, surely, they were just boys when I was at the village last. "My father," the tallest of the group called out. "My father, I am Panther. Do you not remember your son?"

John squinted, shading his eyes from the bright sunshine, and looked at the young brave. "Panther John, it is you," John said embarrassed. "You have become a man. Surely, I have not been gone that long."

"My father, many seasons passed since you here. Come to cabin of sister of my mother. She will have food. We talk."

John followed Panther and the others to the cabin. The Cherokee women, busy with their work, stopped, and looked with curiosity at the white man who came into their town. No one had recognized him. It seemed long ago that he had lived among them. Even his own son did not seem happy to see him. Had he made a mistake to come?

"Redbird," Panther called out. "Redbird Woman, my father return. He hungry. Do you have stew for him?"

Redbird Woman came from behind the cabin, her hands stained yellow from the dye she had been making. She wiped her hands on her apron and smiled, "Yes, Panther, I have food for your father. Welcome John, it good see you," the plump, older woman said.

John returned the smile, thinking that she looked nothing at all like Willow. "Redbird Woman, it is good to see you too. I was afraid no one would remember me."

"Why you wait so long come?" The woman asked, as she dipped hot stew from the iron pot that hung over the fire. "Your son not child now."

"I am sorry. I lost track of time," John said as he took the cup of stew from Redbird Woman.

"You find new woman?" She asked bluntly. "Have more sons, daughters?"

"Yes, I married Agnes. She is gone now. I lost her last year. Left two boys and a little girl with her sister," John answered softly.

"Why John not take care of children?" Redbird Woman asked, frowning. "John not want them?"

John flinched at the acquisitions. He realized that was true, but how could he have taken care of them? He glanced at Panther who had said nothing. "My father, it is my decision to stay with my Cherokee family," Panther said, matter of factly. "You tell me you never forget my mother. You did."

"No, Panther, I have not forgotten your mother or you. That is why I am here," John began, realizing that he had to tell the whole story. "Panther, Redbird Woman, Agnes and her two little boys needed me. I was lonely. I never really loved her." Looking at both of them, he continued. "Willow still haunts me. I still love her."

Redbird Woman shook her head. "Man not live long life loving woman no longer here. Spirit of Willow need let you go." Redbird Woman looked at Panther, "go ask medicine man to meet us at hill of cedars where Willow is buried. Him help John."

John followed Redbird Woman to the hill, a strange feeling instantly came over him. Soon, the medicine man and Panther joined them. To John's surprise, this was the same old medicine man who had tried in vain to save Willow's life. "Ah, John," the feeble old man said in greeting. "I knew you return. Spirit of Willow strong. I help." The medicine man sat on a big rock. "Come sit," he said, taking John's hand. He closed his eyes and began speaking softly in the beautiful language of the Cherokee. John recognized his own name and that of Willow's. The old man became silent waving his free arm toward the brilliant blue sky. Opening his eyes, he looked at John. "The spirit of Willow at rest now. John remember her but move on with life and be happy."

"Thank you," John said to the old medicine man as he looked at the grave of Willow. "I will always remember the love we shared, and I feel that she is at peace now and I am too." He remembered the words of Preacher Daniel, and how they were so similar to the words of the old medicine man.

John stayed in the Cherokee town for a few days, spending time with Panther and Redbird Woman. He realized that he would never again be comfortable with the Cherokee and it was time for him to move on. He had asked Panther to come with him, but his son had said no. He would soon undergo rituals to become a Cherokee Warrior. Panther had promised that he would visit his father in the white man town soon, but he had no desire to live as a white man. He was a Cherokee.

Chapter 24
1754
New Friends

John returned to the settlement of his family. He enjoyed spending time with his now aging older brothers and sisters. Having no home of his own, he lived with Sarah and Denne, sleeping in the lean-to attached to their cabin. He was at peace. Whatever the old priest-medicine man had done seemed to be working. John could think of his life with Willow and the Cherokee people with happiness and realized that part of this life was over. He was considering going to see his children that he and Agnes had together. He still could not understand why he had married a woman he did not love. That too was a part of his life that was over.

The October morning dawned clear and cool. This was the day John had decided he would go in search of the two little boys and the little girl he had left behind. Absalom and Choice were the boy's names and the little girl was called Mary. Would they remember him he wondered? They had been so young when he had left them. No, he thought abandoned was a better word. He had abandoned his children. How could he have done that? He knew the sister of Agnes had taken care of them; she was a good woman too. But they were his children.

John was startled at the number of new settlements that had popped up in every valley. Talking with the residents of these settlements, John had heard rumor of discontent. "We should have our own country," some had said. "We should not be ruled by a king so far away." Having spent time among the Cherokee he had also wondered what would become of them. What would happen when the white man outnumbered the people who had lived there first?

John reached the settlement where the people had treated him so kindly and as luck would have it, it was Sunday, and time for the worship service to begin. Just as the congregation stood to sing, John walked in, and removed his hat, joining with them in song. Preacher Daniel nodded at him and many, including Mary turned and smiled. Preacher Daniel's sermon was moving, and John knew he had done the right thing by coming back and going to see his children.

After the service was over, he was welcomed by the church folks and Mary invited him to her house for dinner. She had just the night before, made a big pot of rabbit stew and oh yes, she had said, an apple pie made from dried apples that she promised would be very good. John could not refuse this nice woman's invitation.

As Mary had said, the food was delicious. John had helped her clean the table and afterwards the two of them sat on the outside bench in the warm sunshine. "John, it is so good to see you again," Mary said, smiling at him. "Where are you heading now?"

"Mary, I am going to see my children. I feel that I have abandoned them and that is not right," John answered. "I do not know what their reaction to me will be. They may not remember who I am or the aunt they are living with also might not let me see them."

Mary nodded, "that is still the right thing to do. When do you go?"

"Probably should be leaving about now. Don't know if I can make it all the way before dark," John said.

"You could stay with Preacher Daniel tonight and leave in the morning," Mary offered.

"Don't want to be any trouble to anybody," John replied.

"You won't be," the preacher said as he came from around the corner of the house. "I think that's an excellent idea," he continued. "I want to find out how things worked out with your son and Willow."

Pulling up a cane back chair, he sat down, looking intently at John. "John, you look more at peace. Did you find the solution to your situation?"

"Yes, yes I did, Preacher Daniel." John began, "The sister

of Willow arranged for the old medicine man to help me. Not sure what he did exactly, but we went to the grave of Willow. He took my hand in one of his, and with the other waved toward the heavens and spoke in the ancient tongue of his people." John paused, mist forming in his eyes. "Preacher Daniel, he said almost the same words that you did and when he finished, instantly I was at peace."

"John, sometimes things are hard to understand, but trusting in God is always the answer. I am happy for you now. What about your son," Preacher Daniel asked?

"The name of my son is Panther. He told me that he will visit me, but that he is Cherokee," John answered. "I promised his mother that I would let him make his choice. He did. I am not sure if I will ever return to the Cherokee town. It is different now. With the exception of Panther, the people I knew and loved are gone." John paused, "Now, I guess, I can move on with my life."

John, Mary and the preacher continued to talk until the sun began to set in the western horizon. The three of them had learned much about each other and a deep bond was beginning to form. John learned that the preacher's wife and young son were visiting her parents in a nearby settlement, and that an older daughter two summer ago had passed away from yellow fever. Mary had her share of sadness also as her husband and son both were killed several years ago by Congaree Indians as they cleared a relative's land. She was a strong woman and was resolved to make the best of what life offered her, always cheerful and ready to help anyone in need.

"Well Mary," Preacher Daniel said, leaning back in his chair. "Looks like me and John need to be heading on over to my cabin. It will be dark pretty soon, and I'll need to round us up some supper."

Mary smiled, her face lighting up, I think not Preacher Daniel. I have plenty food left from dinner. You and John are going to eat with me."

Preacher Daniel laughed, "Why Mary, you know that will be

wonderful. Do you happen to have some of your pie left?"

"Sure do. I will need to fix up a fresh tin of cornbread. While I do that, I'd be most appreciative if the two of you would bring in a few sticks of firewood and," she smiled, "I am running a little low on water."

"At your service mam," Preacher Daniel said, picking up the water bucket.

John smiled at his new friends, finding himself truly happy for the first time in a long, long while.

Chapter 25
Absalom, Choice and Mary

John waved at Mary and Preacher Daniel as he left the next morning. Mary had insisted that he and the preacher come by for breakfast. She had placed on his plate the biggest biscuit and slice of ham covered with apple jelly that he had had since his Mama Joyce had cooked him breakfast many years ago. She poured him a huge mug of strong, sweet coffee that was just as good as Preacher Daniel had said it would be. Mary was a mighty good cook, he thought to himself, and she was right pretty too. She had made him promise that he would come back as soon as he could. She wanted to know about the children.

John reached the little settlement just about midday. Most of the folks were inside eating their noon meal or taking a break from the morning work. He rode slowly on the wide path that served as a road until he found the little cabin of Agnes' sister Martha and her husband. He heard the sounds of several children as he stepped on to the porch. "Hello," he called out. "Hello Martha, I'm John Griffin."

A not so young woman in a faded dress holding a small baby came to the door. Four wide-eyed children and two slightly older boys followed her. "John Griffin," it is you," the woman said. "Thought you were never coming back."

John smiled, looking at the children, not knowing for sure which ones were his. "Yes, I'm back. I had to come see my children."

"Glad you did," Martha said in a tired voice. "John, come meet your children. The tall one is Absalom, he is six. Choice here is almost four," she said, touching the wide-eyed boy's shoulder. "And this pretty little girl is Mary. She is two," she smiled. "The older one over there and of course the baby are mine and the sons of Agnes are helping my husband out in the field."

John's children shyly looked at him and finally the oldest

said, "I remember you. You let me ride on your back like a pony. Aunt Martha said you ain't never coming back." Choice slowly walked over and touched his father's leg as if he was trying to remember and little Mary burst out in tears. John stood and looked at his children in bewilderment. What did he expect? They had been very young when he had left them.

"Hush now Mary," Martha said sweetly. "This here is your Pa." Then looking at John, she continued. "I'll fix you something to eat. Then we've got to have a talk."

After John had eaten a plate of beans and cornbread, Martha put the baby and Mary down on a quilt on the floor and told her son to take the boys out back to play. "John, I'm glad you came back." Martha looked at him kindly. "John, I'm sorry, but I can't keep all of your children. We's poor John. There's times we barely have enough to eat." John listened, expecting to hear this from Martha. "Me and Tom done talked it over. If you can take the boys, I think we can keep Mary. I am sorry, John, but they are yours. I mean…"

"I understand Martha. I don't have a home now. I ain't got no place to take'em. But if you will give me a week or two, I'll be back for'em. I would appreciate it if you could keep the little girl at least for a little while," John answered. John patted the arm of the sleeping little girl and went out back and talked with boys for a few minutes and told them he would be back soon to take them home. He thanked Martha and told her he would return.

John wasn't sure what he was going to do. He reckoned he could go back and live near Sarah and Denne, but something told him he would be happier to build a cabin for himself and the boys at the settlement where preacher Daniel and Mary lived. He would go back there and see what they thought about that idea. The following day, John spoke with Preacher Daniel and Mary.

"Of course, John," Mary said happily. "That would be good, very good."

"We'll get started on your cabin first thing in the morning!" Preacher Daniel exclaimed. There's a piece of land right by me that has an open space in the center that will be just right for a cabin."

John smiled at his new friends. "I was hoping you would like the idea."

"Yes, and we all can help with the boys," Mary said. "And if you decide to bring little Mary back, I will certainly help you with her too. Oh, this will be so much fun. I love children."

A few days later John, Mary and Preacher Daniel stood back and proudly admired the new cabin. With the help of all the settlement men and the women supplying food the little cabin had been quickly completed. John would leave before sunup the following day to bring his children home.

Chapter 26
Truly Blessed

Martha, the aunt of John's children had the boys ready to go when he returned. The boys were excited but also frightened, they did not know their father. After strapping the cloth bag, that held their meager belongings to the back of the saddle, John placed one boy in front of the other and then climbed onto the horse. Martha sadly waved at the boys who waved back, not fully understanding what was happening. Martha said she would miss the boys, but it was for the best. John had told her he would be back for the little girl in two or three months. He had tried to hold little Mary, but she had shied away from him and began to cry. He wondered if the child cried all the time. He would ask his new friend Mary about that; she would know what to do. She seemed to know most everything. John smiled just thinking about her. She had a way about her that made him smile.

Everyone in the settlement came out to meet John and the children. The women had furnished the cabin with a bed for John and a table with four chairs by the fireplace. A ladder led to the loft where corn shuck cots had been placed on the floor for the boys. The shelf in the kitchen contained enough dishes and pots for cooking and eating. There were even clay containers holding ground corn, flour and sugar and another filled with coffee. John could not believe what he saw. He looked from the preacher to Mary, realizing the two of them had been responsible for planning this. John was overwhelmed and felt the love they had for him. He knew he would be happy here.

Mary had as usual told John that he and the boys would have supper with her. The preacher's family had returned so he would go to his cabin for his meal but told John he would see him before bedtime. He felt the need for prayer. The boys instantly took a liking to Mary and she to them. Before supper was over, they were talking to her like they had always known her. They seemed to be a little shy with John, but he knew they would come around.

"Thank you, Mary," John said as he hugged her. "Thank you for everything. You have made a big difference in my life."

"John, I think you have changed mine too," Mary answered, tears gleaming in her eyes. "I love your boys already," she smiled at him, their eyes locking briefly. And to herself, she thought, and I think I love you too.

The boys had been delighted with their new beds. John heard them laughing as he answered the door to let Preacher Daniel in. "Sounds like the boys are happy," Preacher Daniel said, smiling.

"Yes, it does. I hope they settle in quickly," John answered.

"I think they will. Mary and I, and the whole settlement will see to it," Preacher Daniel proclaimed.

"Thank you, Preacher Daniel," John answered. "Please, come sit down. I would offer you something, but I have not had anytime to prepare anything yet. Mary has supplied food for us," John laughed. "She is quite a woman."

"Yes, she is. John, I know you are exhausted, and need to sleep, but I want to pray with and for you."

John nodded as both sat down. "Yes, Preacher Daniel, please do."

Preacher Daniel took the hand of John and began. "Dear Lord, God, please bless this man in the new endeavors of his life. Help him to be a good father and find happiness here with us." He continued on praying for the boys and little Mary who he knew would join them soon. He asked God's guidance for John's son Panther and finished by saying, "Dear God again, I ask for you to grant this man happiness. These things I ask in Jesus name, Amen."

The two men shook hands and John retired in his new bed, and his new home, and knew that he would be truly blessed in this place.

Chapter 27
"Yes, John"

The afternoon was cool with the threat of rain, and the boys much to their dismay were forced to stay inside. Both were settling into their new routine and becoming accustomed to John as their father. He had fried bread for their midday meal, putting bits of dried apple in the mixture as Willow had done years before. The boys watched him in amazement, and asked question after question. "Pa," Absalom asked, "How'd you learn to cook bread like this? It is good."

"Good, good," Choice said, mimicking his brother, holding out his hand for more.

"Well, you see boys," John began, "A Cherokee woman showed me how to make bread."

"Ah, Cherokee, Pa, really!" Absalom exclaimed.

"Yes, at one time I lived with them," John answered, smiling.

"They didn't scalp you?" Absalom asked in disbelief looking up at his father's head.

"No, no, they didn't harm me at all. In fact, they liked me. They liked me a lot," John answered, laughing.

"Awe Pa, you just joking me. You ain't never lived with no Injuns," the little boy stated.

Hearing the word Injuns, Choice began running around the room, shouting, "Injuns, Injuns."

Realizing the fear, the child had for Indians, John knew he had to calm him down. "Choice, Choice, it's alright. There are no Injuns around," John said, pulling the little boy close to him. "Come over here Absalom, I need to tell you boys a story, a true story." Both boys sat down by John's chair and looked expectantly up at their father. "I really did live with the Cherokee. I took a beautiful maiden for my wife." Absalom's eyes widened and Choice had already become distracted by the falling raindrops. John could think of Willow now as a happy memory. He told his sons of the happiness they had known and how he learned the way of the Cherokee. "We had a son."

"Pa," Absalom interrupted, "Pa, I have a brother that's and Injun?"

"No, Absalom," John corrected. "He's not an Injun, he is a Cherokee. His name is Panther, and I am very proud of him."

Absalom sat in silence for a few minutes, trying to understand the things his Pa had said. "Pa, can we see him? Do you think he will like me? Do you think he will show me how to shoot his bow and arrow?"

John smiled, happy that his young son was excited about having a Cherokee brother. "Yes, Absalom," John answered. "One day soon, you can see him. I think he will like you and I bet he will show you how to shoot his bow and arrow." He tasseled the blond hair of his son, "and maybe he'll make one for your very own."

"Me too! Me too!" Choice shouted, not knowing what he was asking for.

"Yes, you too Choice. Let's finish our meal and you boys can help me clean up. Then we'll go over to see Miss Mary. How would you like that," John asked?

"Yea, yea," both boys shouted. They had only been here for a month and already loved Mary and she was wonderful with them.

The rain had stopped, and the temperature had begun to drop when John and the boys headed over to visit Mary. He knew she would have something special for them, she always did. They could smell the scent of freshly baked bread before they reached her cabin. "Mary, Mary," John called out.

"John, you all come on in. My goodness, it's a little nippy out there," Mary said as she opened the door. "Hello boys," she said, bending over to hug both of them. "I'm so glad to see you. I just made bread and later on we can spread honey on it if you like," she said smiling at John over the heads of the children.

John noticed how pretty she looked, and also that she was wearing a dress he had not seen before. "Mary, you look pretty today. When did you have time to make that dress? It is very nice."

Mary's face turned pink. She was hoping he would notice but found herself embarrassed when he had. "Why John, thank you. I had this dress for ages. Ah, just decided that I would wear it today," she replied. She quickly turned to the boys, but not before she and John's eyes met and in that second, they both knew.

"Mary, your right, I believe the weather is a change'n," John answered, embarrassed a little himself. "I think me, and Absalom will go out, and cut a little firewood for you," looking at Choice who was busy stacking little blocks of wood that someone had carved for him. He continued, "Choice you stay here with Miss Mary. Me and Absalom will be back in a little bit."

John and the boys stayed the afternoon with Mary. After cutting and chopping firewood, John brought in water and finally sat down in front of the fire, rubbing his hands together. "Gonna be cold tonight Mary, is there anything else I can do for you," John asked looking at Mary, thinking again how pretty she looked.

"Yes, you and the boys can set yourself down and eat supper with me. Choice and me been cooking up something special while you worked this afternoon. Preacher Daniel killed a rabbit this morning and brought it to me." She sat the just-cooked rabbit on the table, the aroma was tantalizing. "Absalom, get the honey from the shelf and we'll be all set to eat."

After the delicious supper and the dishes had been cleaned, John and the boys prepared to leave. John looked at Mary, "Mary, would you like to walk home with us? I would like to talk with you some more after I put the boys to bed?"

"Yes, john, that would be nice. I'll just get my wrap," Mary said, wondering what he wanted to talk with her about. Could it be? No, she wouldn't dare get her hopes up.

John stirred the fire and both he and Mary hugged the boys and they scrambled up the ladder to the loft. "Good night Miss Mary," Absalom yelled with Choice quickly echoing his brother. "Good night Pa," both boys said in unison. After giggling for a few minutes, the boys became silent and were soon fast asleep.

John pulled two chairs closer to the fire and he and Mary sat down. John looked into the flickering flames and then turned to Mary. "Thank you for helping me with the boys. I could not manage this without your help."

"John, I enjoy the boys," Mary replied, her heart beating a little faster.

"Mary, you know I've got to go get my little girl soon," John said, taking her hand.

Mary nodded, hoping that he couldn't feel her hand shaking inside his. "Mary, will you go with me to get her?"

She nodded again, trying to hide her disappointment. "Of course, John, you know I will."

Mary, ah," John hesitated. "Mary, may I kiss you?"

Mary smiled, leaned her cheek toward the man who pulled her close to him. "Not like that, like this." John took her in his arms and kissed her. "Been wanting to do that for a long time," John said at her response.

"I been wanting you to do that for a long time. John, would it be improper if I said that I love you," Mary asked, trying to hold back the tears that threatened to flow.

"No mam, it wouldn't, cause I love you too. Mary, it would be improper for a man and woman to go sashaying around the countryside if'n they weren't married." John kissed her again. "Mary, will you marry me? Wait before you answer. I need to say something first. I have four children. Three of them need a Ma and the other is part Indian. You know that story. I loved his mother very much. I was young then. And it was a different kind of love. Then I married a woman I did not love." He smiled; you know all about that too. Now, I'm older and I want to spend the rest of my life with you. Mary, I am not asking you this because my children need a ma. I'm asking you simply because I love you. I want to make you happy and I know that you will make me happy. Now, I ask you again, Mary will you marry me?"

"Yes! John, yes!" Mary exclaimed, this time letting the pinned-up tears fall as John kissed her again.

Chapter 28
Husband and Wife

Preacher Daniel married John and Mary the next week in the overflowing little church. Mary was beautiful and so was the dress the settlement women had made for her. One of the women had fashioned her long wheat-colored hair into curls, placing late season wildflowers around her beaming face. The group clapped and cheered when Preacher Daniel pronounced them husband and wife. Afterwards everyone gathered around the wooden tables near the old cedar trees spreading the delicious food the women had spent the morning preparing. The bright sunshine warmed the chilly fall afternoon adding to the festivities. When the celebration was over, John and Mary, still holding hands stopped short when the wind began to blow and as it had happened before during the sad times, the cedars began to sway and seemed to whisper John and Mary, John and Mary. Preacher Daniel had heard this too and assured them it was a sign of happiness and love. John and Mary were ecstatic.

Two weeks later, John and Mary left the boys with Preacher Daniel and his wife while they went to get little Mary. They had borrowed the preacher's two-seat buggy to make the trip and Mary had packed bread and ham that they would eat along the way. Mary was excited to bring the child home, but John still had reservations, every time he had seen the child, she had cried. He was afraid she didn't like him, or she was sick or something. "John, everything will be fine, the baby just needs to know that she is loved, and we have plenty of love to share," she said snuggling closer to her husband.

John turned to his wife and kissed her. "Mary you are right. We do have plenty love and you are a wonderful woman. I never thought that I would find someone like you."

The two of them had an enjoyable trip and reached the settlement just before nightfall. Martha met them at the door holding her baby with John's child following close behind.

"John, I didn't know for sure if you were coming back," Martha said, eyeing Mary. "It won't take long to pack her things." Looking at the pitiful little girl she continued, "Mary you remember, this here is your Pa and this woman is," she paused.

"This woman is my wife and little Mary's new mother," John said, looking at the child who immediately began to cry.

Martha's cool demeanor became even more so. "I'll get the child's things," she said as she turned away muttering to herself. "Well, it didn't take long," she whispered under her breath returning with a small sack of clothing and a worn blanket. "This here's all the child's got. I would give you something to eat before you go but I've barely got enough for me and mine." She turned to the child and briefly held her close. "Bye now, little Mary, you be good." The bewildered child looked at Martha and began to cry even harder. "Oh, tell the boys I miss them," Martha said as she closed the door.

John and Mary looked at each other and both laughed, "How would you like to take a ride in the moonlight Miss Mary," John asked? "I wasn't expecting her to be very nice, but I didn't think she would act like that!"

Mary had picked up the child and was holding her close, talking to her softly, "It's alright little Mary, it's alright. I think a moonlight ride would be wonderful my husband," she answered. "Sure, glad I brought blankets and we still have some bread. We'll be fine, just fine."

The bright moon had risen high in the sky, casting light on the path that was just wide enough for the little buggy. They stopped once in a meadow and ate their bread and drank water from a small nearby stream. The fall night was cool but not uncomfortable. The night sounds of the hoot owl and coyote were pleasant, but John had reached for his old musket when they heard the cry of a bobcat coming a little too close. The child had stopped crying and was soon sleeping soundly in Mary's lap wrapped in her little blanket. John turn to Mary and smiled, "I love you Mary Griffin," he said as they started the final part of their journey.

The night sky was beginning to show signs of the new day when they arrived back home. Mary had moved her belongings into John's new and larger cabin a few days earlier. They would need the space now that all the children were here, and John secretly hoped that Mary could have at least one baby. He was so happy with his new life and loved his wife immensely.

Soon John and Mary and the children were settled into a routine. The boys loved Mary but enjoyed spending time with John as well. Little Mary responded to the love Mary showed her and even warmed up to her father. They were happy.

Chapter 29
Panther's Visit

Time passed quickly and soon five winters had gone by. John had added a new room and a back stoop to the cabin, but he and Mary never had children of their own. Mary had cried, but told John as far as she was concerned, his children were hers.

The settlement had continued to grow with Preacher Daniel saving many souls. He had said it was time to have a revival at the church and invite others to come and learn of the Gospel. They would have several days of service culminating with a big social. He asked the men to hunt for deer and rabbit and for the women to start baking breads and pies. The worship service would start on Wednesday next with the social on the following Saturday. Word had been spread to all of the nearby settlements, many of which had no church or preacher. Preacher Daniel and all the folks were excited for the revival to begin.

Each day as word was spread, more and more people came from the neighboring settlements to hear the comforting message of Preacher Daniel. The church overflowed and the weather was nice, so it was decided to quickly build a brush arbor for the Friday service.

John and Mary, as part of the official welcoming committee had become friendly with a family visiting from several miles away. John had noticed immediately that Gideon Bunch and his pretty daughter were obviously not white although his wife appeared to be. After talking with the family, John had discovered that Gideon's father was a Saponi Indian, a small tribe that lived near the coast. The two of them became quick friends and were sitting together talking before the service began. Other people were still arriving, and John had not noticed the dark-skinned young man dressed in a mixture of Indian and White clothing until he stood in front of him. John looked up at him and said, "Welcome, thank," he paused, "Panther John," John exclaimed. "Panther John," John jumped from the log bench and grabbed his son in a bear hug. "Oh my, oh my," he hugged his son again with tears streaming down his cheek. "What are you doing here?" John had not been back to the Cherokee town in many years and had not seen his son.

"My father," Panther said smiling. "I wanted to see you."

John stepped back and looked at his son. "Panther, you are a man now and you are wearing the clothing of the white man."

"Yes, I was told to wear white man's clothing," he laughed. "Didn't want to be accused of being an Injun."

"And you speak such good English," John stated.

"Spent time with traders and other white men," Panther replied. "You taught me the importance of speaking and understanding the talk of the white man."

Mary cleared her throat and smiled at John, "John, aren't you going to introduce me to your son?"

"Oh yes," John stammered. "Mary, I am proud for you to meet my son, Panther John. And Panther, this is my wife, Mary. And these young'uns here are my children. Absalom, Choice and Little Mary."

Mary immediately hugged the young man and standing on tip toes, kissed his brown cheek. "Panther John, I am delighted to finally meet you. I have heard so much about you. You can call me Mary or if you want, Ma," Mary said happily. The boys looked at their half brother in amazement and Little Mary, still shy, inched behind Mary's skirt.

"Hello Mary," Panther said, smiling as he hugged her. "Maybe I will call you Ma someday. Hello boys," and looking behind Mary to the little girl, he touched her blonde hair and smiled again.

"And," John said, "These are our new friends, Gideon Bunch and his family. I ah think they have something in common with you."

Before any further introductions could be made, Preacher Daniel moved to the front of the arbor. Everyone shifted, making room for Panther. He found himself sitting by Gideon's daughter, Miles. The two young people looked one another and smiled.

Preacher Daniel loudly called out, "Welcome everyone, welcome to our service today. Thank you all for coming. Please join me now in song as we praise our Lord." In his deep voice he began to sing, and others joined in, "All Hail the Power of Jesus Name."

After the service, John invited his new friends to join him and his family for supper. He knew Mary had a big pot of rabbit stew and freshly baked bread and there would be plenty. Panther was the center of attention as he told them of his desire to see how his white family lived and to spend time with them. Gideon entered the conversation saying that he too had the same desire and it seemed to work best to intermingle the two cultures. He was after all, both. Panther had agreed with him and the two formed an immediate friendship.

The families enjoyed the meal and time together and talked until the sun had sunk low below the western horizon. Mary suggested they stay for the final service and social the following day. She told them it would be no trouble at all to prepare a place for them to sleep in the lean to that John had finished just last week. Panther said he would sleep on the floor near the fire. With arrangements made, the families continued to talk well into the night.

When Mary, who seemed never to tire, and John had settled down for the night she told him how happy she was to have Panther here with them and she hoped that he would stay. "And also, did you notice," She added, "that he and Miles continued to glance at each other." Mary in her knowing way smiled, "and wouldn't it be something? Good night John, I love you."

Mary was up well before sunrise the next day and Gideon's wife, who's name was also Mary soon joined her. Talking and laughing, the two women prepared breakfast for their families. Mary had noticed that Panther was not in his place by the fire and wondered where he had gone. Just before the food was ready to be served, Panther and Miles came in together.

"Morning Panther, morning Miles," Mary greeted them. "My goodness, the two of you are up and about early this morning."

"Yes, Mary," Panther said smiling. "I went out early to watch the new day begin and I bumped into Miles."

"We watched together," Miles added. "Seeing the new day is a special time for me,"
She looked at Panther and smiled and the two Marys smiled also.

Preacher Daniel had delivered an inspiring message and ended by saying, "Paise the Lord. Now please join me in singing Rock of Ages." The little congregation joyfully sang and then were dismissed, everyone being invited to the attend the fellowship social. Food was spread on long log tables beside what the settlement folks now called Whispering Cedars. The cedars remained silent on this day as the soft wind blew serene and peaceful. The warm afternoon was enjoyed and was over much too quickly. Souls had been saved and new friends made, but it was time for the visitors to return to their homes.

Panther John and Miles had spent as much time together as possible and it was very obvious that the two were attracted to each other. Both Marys had known that from the start. The two young people stood off to the side while John and Gideon shook hand and the women hugged each other. "My new friends," John began, "We will have to visit each other often. I feel that we have always known each other."

"Yes, that is true. And we will come see you all and you must come visit us," Gideon answered.

"Mr. Bunch," Panther said hesitantly, "I am not sure how to do this. I have been told that white people do things differently from Indians. But sir," he paused. "Sir, may I have your permission to come visit Miles? Mr. Bunch, I really like her," Panther finished awkwardly.

Both Marys smiled and Gideon shook his head, "Of course, Son, if that's what Miles would like, then it's fine with me."

John and his family walked to the edge of the settlement waving goodbye to the Bunch family. As they passed by the cedars, the sun slid from behind the light feathery clouds and the whispering cedars seemed to sweetly sing in the soft breeze.

Chapter 30
A Different Ceremony

John and Mary enjoyed spending time with Panther, and the boys idolized him. He had made both boys a bow and showed them how to fashion arrowheads from stone. Little Mary had kissed his check when he made a Cherokee doll for her.

When three weeks had passed, Panther announced that he would like to go visit Miles and that he would like John and Mary to go with him as well. Preacher Daniel had volunteered to let little Mary stay with him and his wife, as the child feared new people and places. John, Mary, Panther and the boys left the following morning, and planned to return in a couple of days. Panther was nervous and excited about seeing Miles again. John told him he had felt the same long years ago when he had fallen in love with his mother Willow. The three of them had laughed when Mary had given him words of wisdom.

The Bunch family were happy to see John, and Mary and Miles blushed, her dark face beaming when she saw Panther. He took her hand, and the two of them walked down the path by a sparkling little stream. The families enjoyed the visit, and Gideon promised that they would come some to see them. They wanted to hear another message from Preacher Daniel as well. He was such a nice man. Gideon's wife Mary had proclaimed. Panther disappointed his father and Mary when he told them his decision to go back north to the Cherokee town.

Mary had threatened to cry exclaiming, "Panther, I really enjoy you being with us. Can you come back soon?"

Panther smiled and looked at Miles, remembering the kiss they had just shared. "I will be back soon, very soon Miss Mary," he couldn't quite bring himself to call her Ma, not just yet. "I have some very important things to take care of first."

John, Mary and the boys went south back to the settlement, and Panther went north. John wondered if the important things Panther needed to take care of had anything to do with a wedding ceremony. Indeed, John had been correct. Panther and Miles had declared their love for each other and wanted Preacher Daniel to perform the wedding before the ground was white with snow. They both had agreed to a white Christian ceremony, but also one that included their native heritage. Afterall, both of them were part Indian. John, and Gideon and both Marys had been happy for their children and were excited for them. Preacher Daniel had said that it would be appropriate to intermingle a Christian and Indian ceremony.

For the next three weeks, Panther had spent time between his Cherokee home, and the settlement of John and Mary and that of Miles. He had taken Miles to visit Redbird Woman, the sister of his mother. At first sight the two had hugged each other forming an instant bond. Redbird Woman had told Panther that his mother would have approved his choice of a wife. She had been delighted when she was told that she would go to John's settlement for the wedding ceremony and celebration.

The gold and orange leaves sparkled in the autumn sun, and everyone in the settlement turned out for the unusual wedding which would take place on the hill near the old cedars. Mary was honored when Panther asked her to walk by his side to represent his white mother. Redbird Woman would be on his other side representing Willow his Cherokee mother. Miles' mother Mary would be at her side, all three women holding the brightly colored blankets that would be exchanged by Panther and Miles.

When Preacher Daniel approached and turned to face them the excited audience became silent. "Welcome," he said. "Thank you all for coming to witness the joining of Panther John and Miles in holy matrimony. Today's ceremony will be somewhat different from other wedding ceremonies you have seen. Today we will blend the white Christian ceremony with that of the Cherokee." He nodded and Panther John and his mothers came in stood in front of Preacher Daniel. Then Miles and her mother did the same. The blankets were given to Panther John and Miles and the women moved to the side. The couple looked deeply into each other's eyes as Preacher Daniel spoke, telling them of the promises they were making to love and honor each other in the presence not only the people attending the ceremony but more importantly the Lord. Panther John gave Miles his blankets and she gave him hers. At their feet lay previously roasted deer and bread made from corn. These were exchanged solemnly. Redbird Woman and Miles' mother stepped forward and retrieved the items. Panther John and Miles joined hands and Preacher Daniel smiled, "I now pronounce you man and wife. Panther John you may kiss your wife."

The audience erupted in loud cheers when Panther kissed Miles, and unexpectedly the sweet sound of music filled the air as Mile's father began to play his wooden flute. The old cedars began to sway, and again seemed to softly whisper their song.

Chapter 31
John Was a Good Man

Panther and Miles had made the decision to make their home in the settlement of Mile's father and mother. The settlement was centrally located between the Cherokee village of Panther to the north, and the home of his father to the south. Folks from both white settlements had all pitched in to clear the land and build a cabin for the newlyweds. Panther was not at all surprised when two large skinned deer and three turkeys and also a brown reed basket filled with dried corn mysteriously appeared at the partially built cabin two days after the ceremony.

"Where did this come from Panther?" Miles asked confused but delighted.

"My Cherokee family," Panther answered as he took his wife's hand. "You do know we will go there often."

"Of course, and we will also go to the Saponi town of my father. We still have family there," Miles answered as she stood on her tip toes to kiss the cheek of her husband. "Family is so important, and we need to cherish and remember the heritage we received from them."

The cabin was quickly finished, and all the settlement people were invited for a big party. The women contributed fall vegetables with bread made from corn and all sorts of pies and cakes. This with the deer and turkey supplied by Panther's family was plenty for all. Several men brought their fiddles, and a few had little clay jars filled with corn mash liquor tucked inside their coats. Preacher Daniel just smiled and turned the other way. The eating, hand clapping and dancing lasted until the sun began to fade into the horizon. Some of the settlement folks had said that was the most fun they had had in a long time.

* * * * * * * *

The years quickly passed, and Panther John and Miles were happy, going often to the settlements of John and Mary and also to the villages of the Cherokee and Saponi. Both wanted their children, and there were four of them, one girl, three boys, one of them named John, to know their Indian families, although they were raised as white.

Other mixed families did not share the same sentiment as Panther John and Miles and animosity continued to grow between the two races. This was not the only problem that plagued the colonies now. The mother country of England made more demands expecting them to behave as obedient children. The people of the colonies considered themselves as separate and individual, each with their own ruling power, resenting being told what they could and could not do. Also, the countries of France and Spain continued to claim parts of the country. This situation created a tense mood throughout the colonies. Concerned men gathered at churches and cabins, often talking late into the night. What can we do? This was asked over and over with no one having the answer.

The November day had been cold and cloudy with the threat of snow in the air. The scribbled note hanging on the blacksmith's door urged all the men of the settlement to meet at the church 'bout sundown. It read that an important man from one of the bigger settlements had some talking to do.

John saddled up his old horse, and kissed Mary on the cheek. "Be back soon as I can honey. Spect I'd like to have some hot coffee then," he said, pulling his coat closer. "Looks like we might get some snow."

"Now John," Mary began sweetly. "You be careful now. Wish they'd have them meetings during the daytime. Old men ain't got no business going out on such a night."

"I will Mary. You just keep that fire stirred," John said as he climbed on to his horse.

The meeting was well attended with most of the settlement men, their pipes in hand, listening intently to the speaker. Old Preacher Daniel had started the meeting asking the Lord to help them make good decisions and to bless them all.

A young educated man dress in fancy cloths stood before

them and began to speak. "Thank you, gentlemen."

One of the old men in the back of the church laughed, "We ain't gentlemen, we just plain old men."

The young man smiled, "Well, men I am happy to be here. I will make this talk quick like. The snow is coming, and you need to get back home. You know the King of England is invoking more and more laws on us here in the colonies. He is planning to increase taxes. He plans to tax everything that we buy and sale." The men groaned, one forgetting he was in church, saying a word he should not have said. "And," the young man continued, "He is already sending Redcoat soldiers here to prevent Spain and France from gaining anymore territory, to watch us and to make sure we do not join in with them, and to force the king's laws on us."

The young man quickly finished his talk, and Preacher Daniel asked God to take care of his people. Some of the men, talking among themselves as they put on their coats remarked that a revolution would straighten things out.

John was among the last to leave, wanting a few words with Preacher Daniel. "Preacher Daniel, I think Mary would like for you all to join us on Thanksgiving if you don't have any other plans."

"John, we would be delighted. I'll come by and talk with Mary one day next week. Now, you take care going home," he cautioned, opening the door. "Believe it's starting to sleet."

"I will. Goodnight Preacher Daniel, and I'll tell Mary that you all will come." John pulled himself on to the horse, noticing that the rheumatism in his knees sure did hurt. "Must be this awful weather," he said to himself. John had just passed the cedars on the hill near the cemetery when the howling wind spooked his horse, causing it to rare sharply, throwing John to the ground. John opened his eyes for a moment and heard the old cedar trees call his name. John Griffin was buried the following day in the cemetery underneath the old cedars. Preacher Daniel cried as he said, "John was a good man."

Chapter 32
Cowpens

The settlement nor the lives of John's and Mary's children were never the same after the cold, snowy night of John's accident. Mary, still healthy, continued to live in the cabin he had built for her, with the children keeping her company. Panther John and Miles spent a good deal of time at the Cherokee village. Panther seemed to find solace there among his mother's people.

The situation in the colonies continued to disintegrate. Soon the decisions made in the little country churches and private homes echoed that of the governors and leaders of the colony. A revolution was imminent. More of the Redcoat soldiers sailed from England in big boats and soon infiltrated the colonies. A small portion of the colonist called loyalist did side with the English Parliament. In most cases, the farmers and storekeepers who showed up in their homespun shirts and britches, with muskets in hand, called themselves patriots. These men were ready to fight to form their own government, and most importantly their own country.

While many of the battles took place in the northern colonies, a particularly humiliating battle did take place in the colony of South Carolina. On a cold January day in 1787, twenty-one-year-old Gideon Griffin slipped from his horse, holding tightly to his musket. The orders were to surround the barn where the loyalists were barricaded. Gideon wasn't sure what the plans were, and he knew the group of dragoons did not have enough artillery. He watched in amazement while some of the men took a pine log and fashioned it into what looked like a cannon. The pretend cannon was pointed toward the log buildings, and then Colonel William Washington, a nephew of future president George Washington, yelled out for the men inside to surrender. The Colonel told his dragoons to be prepared to fire on his order. The order did not come, and the loyalist all walked out of the barn in surrender. Gideon smiled and the young man next to him giggled out loud. "Good Lord," Gideon said softly, "we sure fooled them. My Pa, John sure would have been proud of us." A cow lowed as if in agreement. It was a humiliating battle for the British that became known as the Battle of Cowpens.

John Griffin's son Gideon would be a part of several battles of the revolution, but he would never forget this one. Gideon would always smile when his children and grandchildren would ask him to tell the story of how a pine log in a cow pen won the battle without a shot being fired.

The colonial patriots along with valiant soldiers like Gideon persevered and the revolution was won. A new country was born. A new country with its own government, and constitution and most importantly the right to be free from the rule of the British King. This new country flourished, with small settlements becoming towns, and towns becoming cities. The vast open spaces became territories, and then states that all joined together to become the United States of America.

The Griffin family like other people of this county were proud and hardworking. They tilled the land to feed their large families. They were happy and trusted in the Lord to see them through hard times that would come and there would be many.

Chapter 33
Alabama Bound

By 1847 five generations of the Griffin family had made their homes, in first the colony, and then the State of South Carolina. For more than one-hundred fifty years, the family, had lived, loved and died here. Now it seemed the urge to see other places called.

John Griffin, the great grandson of the first John, set at the table in the much larger cabin that he and his second wife Mary Magdalene shared. His first wife had died in childbirth several years earlier. Mary sat his cup of coffee in front of him and smiled as he looked up at her, "Honey, the eggs and bacon are just about ready." John nodded, sipping his coffee, but did not answer. "John, is something wrong" Mary asked, concerned? "No, Mary just heard some interesting talk down at the store yesterday," John answered, taking the plate of bacon and eggs from his wife.

"What kind of talk, John. Was it bad?" Mary asked, sitting down.

"No, no not bad, just some that's got me to thinking. Some of the folks are talking 'bout going down southwest, to Alabama," John answered. "Sweetie, can you get me some of that honey to go on my biscuit?"

"To Alabama?" Mary asked, handing him the honey jar, "What on earth for?"

"Well, there's land, good land available down there, now that all the Creeks and them other Indians have all been moved to Indian Territory. They say, cotton grows mighty good down there. And a change might be good for us," John replied.

"John Griffin, you should be ashamed of yourself!" Mary admonished. "You know them Indians you were talking about are your very own people."

John smiled sheepishly, "You are right, I know Great Grandpa John married Willow, a Cherokee and Grandpa John married Miles. Think she was a Saponi, but all that's changed now.

We live as whites and so did my Ma and Pa."

"So, what's that hanging on the wall?" Mary asked, pointing to a brightly colored, hand-made blanket, "and that basket on the shelf? I know some of your folks came from across the big water, I think England, and also your Ma said that some of your folks came from Germany, but John," Mary stopped, wiping tears from her eyes, she continued. "John, you know that you are part Indian, and I have Indian blood too."

John took Mary's hand in his, "I'm sorry honey. I didn't intend to say anything bad about our people. You know I'm proud to have Indian blood running through my veins. I just think it would be a good thing for us to make this move. We got a little money saved up. Maybe we can find us a good piece of land." "We'll talk about that John," Mary answered. "Now, I need to see to the children."

****

John convinced Mary that moving to Alabama was best for them, and less than a month later, the family, some relatives and friends all packed their belongings into their wagons and headed southwest. They were Alabama bound. In a few days' time, they passed out of South Carolina into the State of Georgia. The Georgia folks were friendly, offering food and water as the Griffin's, and their friends passed by the large cabins. Some of the cabins were two stories high, and others had an open space in the center, a dog trot they were told. Mary had declared that she would like for her new home to be like that. "A fine place to work," She said. "Would keep the rain off and the hot sun too." John had smiled, he already had plans to build them a large dog trot cabin when they reached Alabama.

Some of the kin folks, including John's oldest son, decided to stay in north Georgia while the others moved on. In a remote wooded area, John and Mary noticed the remains where people, not so long ago, had lived. This was a poignant moment for the two of them. All that remained were abandoned log cabins and an occasional pottery jar or bottle, the artistic designs glimmering in the afternoon sunshine.

"Our people once lived here," Mary said sadly. "And now they are gone, leaving on the trail where they cried, never more to return. It is so sad," She finished, tearfully.

"I know," John said softly. "I feel their presence too."

A little girl, her braided black hair hanging down her back, tugged on her mother's apron. "Mama, what people are you talking about?"

"Our people, Rose Anna," Mary answered. "The Cherokee people who lived here."

The child nodded, not truly understanding. "Can I keep this? I found it on the ground." She opened her hand showing a strand of tiny, white beads.

Mary gasped, taking the beads from her daughter's hand. "Yes, yes you can. Rose Anna, my child, it was meant for you to find these. This is a gift from one of the grandmothers," Mary said, placing the strand around the little girl's neck. Looking up at her father, Rose Anna smiled as she skipped off to show her sisters. John looked startled and a chill filled him. For a moment he felt as if he had looked into the face of his great, great grandmother.

Chapter 34
To Find the Tallapoosa

John and Mary and their family continued on, crossing the Georgia line into Alabama. The warm early autumn days and cool nights made travel pleasant. Camping by the majestic Tennessee River for a day or two of rest, the family met another group of travelers also from South Carolina. They were on their way to the western part of Alabama where some family members had already made their homes. The two families became friends, and invited John and Mary to come with them. Winston County would be a good place to live, they had said.

"John," Mary whispered as they pulled their blankets closer. "Just look at the stars. I do believe they shine brighter here in Alabama."

"You know honey, I think you might be right," John said.

"John, are we going west with our new friends? Mary asked. "I thought you said we were going further south, down where the cotton grows tall."

"I did, didn't I," John answered, sliding closer to his wife. "But it might be nice to know somebody when we get there. We can always go down south later. Might depend on the folks and what they think about things. Night Mary, let's get some sleep. We pull out early in the morning."

"Good night, John," Mary answered as a bright light streaked across the night sky. "John, did you see that?" John was already snoring and did not see the star that fell from the heavens.

John was awake before the sun's light begin to shine on the river. He had dreamed of cotton, cotton as tall as his waist. He took this as a sign for him to move on south instead of west. Mary already had bacon frying and coffee ready when her husband placed a kiss on her cheek. "Ready to go south my dear," he asked.

Mary laughed at her husband, "Can't make up your mind, can you? John, I go where you go, but why the change?"

"Dreamed of high cotton last night Mary, and for some reason I can't explain, I feel drawn to the river called the Tallapoosa. Hear tell the valley there is a fine place to live."

"That's where we will go then," Mary answered, handing John a plate of bacon and biscuits. "But let's eat first."

Part of the Griffin family packed up and headed south, while John's sister's family decided to go west to Winston County. John and Mary, after traveling through vast forest of hardwood trees, entered into an area of open meadows covered with orange and yellow fall wildflowers. Soon they reached a broad, fast flowing river.

"John is the river you were talking about. Is this the Tallapoosa?" Mary asked, smiling as a flock of geese flew over the treetops.

"No, don't think so," John answered, pulling the team of mules to a halt. "I was told there would be a bigger river, the Coosa, before we reach the Tallapoosa. Good place to camp though," He said looking around. "That spot behind the trees will do nicely."

"John, Tallapoosa, Coosa, what sort of names are these, anyway?" Mary questioned as she jumped from the wagon. "Don't sound like any of the creeks or rivers back home."

"Mary, this is, I mean was, Creek Indian country. Think it's about the line between the Cherokee and them Creek. It means something I'm sure. We'll find out when we run across a town."

"John, how we gonna get to the other side?" Mary asked as the children gathered around her.

"Was told that once we get near the towns along the river, there'll be ferries. Guest that's what we'll do," John replied. "I'll gather up some firewood for the fire, you start getting food ready to cook. I'm hungry."

After supper was finished and Mary had the children tucked in for the night, she took John's hand. "John let's walk down by the river and sit for a spell afore we lie down for the night.

There's still enough daylight to see and the moon will be coming up soon."

John nodded, "It is pleasant here, ain't it? I spec we're really gonna like it in Alabama." They sat in silence, watching the water rush by, and the sounds of the day ending and the night coming alive. The final call of the brown thrasher was quickly followed by the rapid hoot of the owl and the sharp bark of a lone coyote. Shadows began to fall, and the sun was quickly gone only to be replaced by the big, yellow moon.

"My, how quickly it all changed," Mary whispered, "And now it's getting cold. I think I'm ready to go lie down by the fire under the cover of our blankets."

"Me too, we have a long day ahead of us tomorrow. If we can find a ferry, we'll cross this river and be at the Tallapoosa soon. If we make good time, we should reach our destination in two or three days," John predicted, yawning. "Good night, Mary."

The next morning promised another beautiful day as the sun rose in a cloudless sky. The Griffin's continued, along the small road near the river that was just barely big enough for the wagon to pass. Midday came and went and there was still no sign of a town or ferry.

"Mighty pretty river, John," Mary said. "Sure would be nice to be on the other side though."

"It would, Mary. Didn't know it would take this long to find a ferry," John answered, laughing as he pulled the mules around a curve in the road. "Look Mary, there's a meadow and a plowed field. I think we are coming up on a town and the ferry."

The bustling town of Gadsden was a welcome sight to the Griffin family. John pulled the wagon off to the side of the dusty road and told Mary to keep the children inside the wagon while he went inside the dry goods store for a few supplies and maybe a surprise for the children.

"Pa, can I go with you?" Rose Anna asked, "I be sweet."

John shook his head, "No, baby girl, you stay here with Mama."

"Please Pa?" the little girl begged.

John seemed to have a soft spot for the child, "Oh, alright Rose. Come on now," he said, taking her hand. "You can help me carry the supplies."

"Thank you," Rose Anna said, happily taking her father's hand.

John paid the storekeeper for the flour and sugar along with the coffee and bacon and the hard candy for the children. "Where you head'n?" the man asked kindly.

"South," John answered, placing the candy in Rose Anna's hand. Hold this real tight Rose." Looking up at the man he continued, "Somewhere in the Tallapoosa River Valley. Know any good settlements down that way?"

"Matter of fact, I do," the old fellow answered, bending over to give Rose Anna another piece of candy. 'Sure, is a mighty pretty little girl you've got there. Some kin of mine moved off down there ah while back. Said they liked it. Plenty of open space and soil that'll grow jest 'bout anything. The northern part is a bit hilly though."

"Do you happen to know the name of the town, and which way I need to go to get there?" John asked.

"Name of the town is Dade, ah, Dadeville," he stammered. "Named after a soldier that himself killed down in Floridee fighting them Seminoles. Course they had a big battle 'bout ten miles from the town, think they call the place Horseshoe Bend. Lots of them Injuns got killed there. Too bad, but it opened the door for us white folks to settle Alabama. If you cross the river in the right place, you may see where the battle happened. Anyway, think you go straight south once you cross the river. Reckon it's about two, maybe three days travel. The town's a few miles east of the river.

The man had not noticed when John had flinched when he talked about Indians. "Mighty obliged," John said smiling. "Now Rose Anna tell the nice man thank you for your candy."

"Thank you, bye, bye?" the child said, her dark eyes sparkling in the sunlight.

"Bye, little girl. What's your name," the man asked, thinking the child and the man must be part Indian.

"My name is Rose Anna," she answered proudly.

John paid the ferry man two bits to cross the Coosa River, and the Griffin family was on their way to find the Tallapoosa and Dadeville.

Chapter 35
Startling Experience

The little road curved round and round, going uphill and then down into valleys, making one child and then another sick. "My goodness John, reckon how much longer afore we get to the Tallapoosa?" Mary asked softly. Think I'm gonna be sick too!"

"Hold on Mary," John replied. "Saw flat land and a glimmer of water when we were on top of that last hill. Don't think it will be much longer."

John had been correct, and in only a short time the Tallapoosa came into view. "Oh John," Mary gasped. "What a beautiful river. Even more so than the Coosa."

They followed the river on for several miles deciding to camp early for the night. As they were eating supper by the fire, a young man stopped by, and asked if they could share a little food. He had nothing to eat all day.

"Sure, what's your name and where are you heading?" John asked, extending his hand.

"Name's James Carson, sir," he replied, taking a plate of hot stew from Mary. "Been down to Mobile working at the dock, heading back home to Huntsville. Thank you, mam. Where you folks heading?"

"Want to find some land down around a place called Dadeville. Did you happen to pass that way?" John asked.

"Yes sir, looked like a right good place to go. It's a ways down the road. You need to go ahead and cross the river right down yonder. "Think you can ford there," the young man said, an odd look covering his face. "Had a strange experience right after I crossed. You know there was a big battle real close to here back in 1814 between the white soldiers and the Injuns. Sure, thought I heard'em," he shook his head. "Jest don't know. Thank you, folks, for the good stew. Reckon I'll be on my way. Figure I can make it a few more miles afore dark. Nice to meet you and good luck."

The next morning, happy to be on the last leg of their journey, the Griffin family enjoyed the warm sunshine as they continued down the road to the river. They had not traveled far when an eerie silence seemed to overcome them. The birds had stopped singing, and a grove of cedars trees began to sway in the light breeze and seemed to softly whisper strange names. John and Mary looked at each other, neither speaking. John remembered stories told by his family about whispering cedars. Was that happening here and now? Rose Anna, sitting between her parents, pointed to white stick-like objects lying on the hillside. "Mama, what is that?" She asked softly.

Startled, Mary realized instantly that they were passing the battle site the young man had spoken of, and this was bones of slain warriors. She pulled the child close, shielding her from the site. John quickened the pace of the mules, and moved on as fast as he could, cold chills running down his back. They quickly forwarded the river and traveled in stunned silence. A long time would pass before John and Mary would speak of the whispering cedars.

The Griffin family reached the outskirts of the little town of Dadeville well before sundown. Seeing the sign over the split log store front that read Dry Goods and Land Sales, John jumped from the wagon and tied the mule reins to the hitching post. "Back in a bit, Mary. Keep the young'uns in the wagon."

"After noon," a middle-aged man from behind the counter said as John entered the store building. "What can I do for you?"

"Afternoon," John answered. "Me and my family just arrived here from South Carolina. We're looking for a place to settle and someone back up the way said Dadeville was a good place."

"Well now, you got some good information. What's your name, and how much land to you need?" Pausing he continued, "Oh, by the way, name's Pete, Pete Smith."

"Howdy Pete," John answered, reaching out his hand. "Depends on what the going price is, but I reckon 'bout five or six acres. Like for it to be on a good-sized creek."

"Know the perfect place. If you give me a few minutes to close up, I'll show it to you and then we'll talk about the price. Oh, by the way, the land is out of town aways," Pete said as he grabbed his jacket.

John followed Pete for several miles, the little road becoming smaller, but the countryside was very pretty Mary said. Pete stopped underneath a large oak tree in an open clearing beside the roadway. "Got 'bout six or seven acres here. Creek just down the hill there. Think I can sell it to you fer three and a half dollars an acre," Pete scratched his head, thinking, "that'll be twenty-five dollars cash. If you got the money, I got the deed right here," he said smiling, pulling a piece of paper out of his pocket.

John looked at Mary and returned her smile. "Yep, think this will do just fine. Mary get the money for the man and I'll sign the papers. Pete, how far to the river?"

"You're in luck my friend, this here piece of land joins the river 'bout a quarter mile down that way," Pete said, pointing toward the west. "If I remember right, some Injuns lived there afore they were moved away."

John smiled as he and Pete traded the deed for a bag of silver dollars and the deal was done. The Griffin family would build the large dog-trot house and expand it over the years as their family continued to grow. John would even build a separate log kitchen out behind the cabin. This made Mary very happy.

Chapter 36
The Best Thing to Do

The winds of change blew hard over the southland during the next several years. Others like the Griffins came to Alabama by the droves. Many built their homes of logs in the northern part of the state while others moved further south enjoying the houses that cotton built. The cotton crop was big and important in Alabama, just as it was all across the south. The soft white balls brought both prosperity and destruction and ultimately a change of life. By the early 1860s folks were hearing a new word, but few understood, secession.

John had ridden into town to pick up a pound of sugar, it was one of the young'uns birthday and Mary was going to bake a cake. Shoot, it seemed like one of them had a birthday every month, he laughed to himself as he went into the same store where he had met Pete many years before. Several older men were sitting in cane back chairs listening to a young man talk. Pete saw John and motioned for him to pull up a chair.

"I tell you; secession is the only way to go!" the young man said with anger in his voice.

"What does this word secession mean, exactly?" one of the old men asked, putting a plug of tobacco in his mouth.

"It means sir," the young man answered, "It means that we pull out from the United States along with other southern states and form our own country."

"Why we want to do that?" another old man asked. "I love this country. Why, my Pa fought so we could have this here land."

"My grandfather did too, sir," the young man said respectfully. "Things have changed. Lincoln demands tax money from us. Lots of money. Forty percent to be exact. That's how the rest of the country survives, with tax money from the south. Money from our own cotton sales."

The old men sat in silence, each pondering on what the young fellow had said. Looking around the room, the young man continued. "How many of you have men of color to help you with their crops?"

"You mean slaves" one man asked.

"Why, we ain't got no slaves. Old Rufus and his woman live on my land. They help me when I need it. I giv'em food, and let'm live in the shack without paying. But they ain't slaves. They's part of my family."

Shaking his head, another added, "Same with me. I do know a few folks that's got three or four. They treated good. Spec they could leave if they wanted to."

"That's what I thought," the young man said, smiling. "People up north say it's wrong to have," he paused, "Slaves. They want to set them free, ours here in the south, but not any that belong to them up there."

"I say we do this secession thing," and old man from the back of the room said.

"And I say we don't," another added.

"I think we should be patient and see what happens," Pete chimed in, pushing back his chair.

And so, it went, many in the town of Dadeville and northern parts of the county did not like the idea, while most in the south agreed it was the best thing to do. When all the votes were counted at the convention in Montgomery that had been called by the governor, the county of Tallapoosa had opposed secession, but the State of Alabama as a whole had voted to secede. When the time came to muster up the troops, many from Tallapoosa County were first in line to join.

Chapter 37
Sweet Sad Song of Dixie

The young woman loosely tied her black hair back with a blue ribbon that matched her dress. Looking in the mirror, she smiled at her reflection, her dark eyes twinkling. "Rose Anna, I do declare, you are prettying yourself up jest to go knit a pair of socks," Mima, Rose Anna's oldest sister said smiling. "Why, you'd think you was going to see a fellow."

"Well, I just want to look nice," Rose Anna answered, patting the ribbon in place. "And you know that the streets are just full of soldiers. And they all look so handsome!" Both young ladies laughed as they gathered their knitting baskets and headed out the door. Pa had said he would take them up town today to meet with the other women to knit socks and other items of clothing for the boys and men of the Confederacy. The Tallapoosa County town of Dadeville has also loaned the Confederate government many bales of cotton, a large amount of money as well as wheat and corn. Most folks were happy to help in any way they could for the "Cause." They also thought that the fighting wouldn't last for long.

John pulled the mules to a halt and jumped down to help his daughters from the wagon. As he took Rose Anna's hand a group of soldiers in brown, homespun linen passed by, one bumping into them. "Excuse me sir, mam," a tall man who seemed a little older than the others said, tipping his cap, as he looked at Rose Anna and smiled.

"That's quite alright soldier," John answered. "What unit are you boys in?"

"Company B, 1st Alabama State Troops, sir," the soldier replied as he walked on down the street.

"Oh, he was so handsome," Rose Anna whispered to her sister. "And he had a nice smile too!"

"Oh, come on Rose, we're going to be late," Mima said, laughing, grabbing Rose Anna's hand. "Pa," she continued, "Come back for us about midafternoon."

Rose Anna and the young man would bump into each other again at church on the following Sunday, both immediately recognizing each other. "Excuse me again mam," he said warmly. "My name is Bert, Bert Williams. May I ask what your name is?"

Hello, Bert, my name is Rose Anna Griffin," she said sweetly.

"Nice to see you again, mam," Bert replied, sitting down on the wooden pew.

Rose Anna smiled as she followed her family across the aisle and sat down. Many times, during the service her dark cheeks turned pink as she glanced over her shoulder to see Bert watching her.

In early August 1862, amid the hustle and preparation of going to war, Bert and Rose Anna were quietly married on the steps of the little Methodist Church in the town of Dadeville. The sweet scent of cedar filled the air, and the redbird happily sang his song as the preacher pronounced them man and wife. Rose Anna had heard the story many times of the whispering cedars during both sad and happy times of many generations of the Griffin family. She was not surprised to hear the whispering now. Bert looked at her in surprise and quietly asked, "Rose, did you hear that sound? Was it coming from the cedar trees?"

"Yes Bert, I heard. I will explain later," Rose Anna answered. Hand in hand the newlyweds walked to their buggy, as someone was heard playing the sad, sweet song of *Dixie* on the violin.

The early emotions and excitement of adventure soon gave way to fear, and dread as tearful women watched as their husbands and sons proudly waving the rebel flag, march off to war. Several Griffin men were among the crowd. The next two years brought death and destruction to the Southland. Many, many men from Alabama including Tallapoosa County never returned to kiss their mothers, their wives and sweethearts nor to till their native soil.

Chapter 38
Floating in the Wind

Bert and Rose moved farther on down the Tallapoosa River to raise their family, and like others endured the hardship of the aftermath of the war. Mary, Rose's mother, took sick with the fever and passed away a year or so after the war ended. Old John lived for several years more in the cabin he had built for Mary many years before. Bert had chosen a plot of land near a creek that some of the old settlers called Menawa Creek, named for the old Creek leader at the Battle of the Horseshoe.

The valley provided fertile soil for corn crops, and garden vegetables, and Bert even tried his luck with upland cotton on the hillside. Rose Anna picked out the perfect site for their home, high on top of one of the hills near a grove of cedar trees. She had said she could hear the soft voices of the cedars speaking to her. At first Bert thought Rose was just imagining things then understood what had drawn her to that particular spot when he heard for himself, the cedars speak.

"Bert," Rose reminded him, "Remember on our wedding day when the cedars spoke to us? I told you one day I would explain. So, I'll fix us a cup of coffee, and let's go sit on the front porch," She smiled at her husband. "How about a piece of that chocolate cake I just baked? I think that now is a good time to tell you the story of the whispering cedars and my family."

Rose Anna rose from her chair, placing her hand on her swollen belly. She hoped the baby came before Thanksgiving, she had so much cooking to do. She cut two pieces of the freshly baked cake and poured steaming coffee into large mugs and placed them on the wooden try that Bert had made for her. She grabbed her shawl and joined Bert outside on the porch.

"Oh, Bert what a beautiful afternoon. I just love the fall." Rose Anna exclaimed, sitting down next to Bert.

"I do too Rose," Bert answered, taking his mug and cake. "But I love your chocolate cake even more. Now, tell me about the story of the whispering cedars."

"Well, it began oh, 'bout a hundred fifty years ago, I reckon," Rose Anna began. "There was a bad storm, a tornado, and my great-great granddaddy John got caught out in it. He managed to get inside and was only slightly injured, but several people in the little village were killed, including a little girl. Her name was Caroline.

They buried the people on the hillside near some cedar trees. After the funeral service was over, the story that was passed down has it that the cedar trees began to sway in the breeze, and softly whisper Caroline." Rose Anna paused; chill bumps visible on her arms. "Bert, I feel like I was there." Bert reached for Rose Anna's hand, realizing that his wife had indeed just experienced an event that had happened long, long ago. "This happened many times throughout the lives of my family. When someone died, the whispering cedars seemed to hold their spirits for a moment before carrying them away. My Pa and Ma told me that when they passed by the place where that battle 'tween the soldiers, and the Indians was fought, they heard the cedars whisper the unfamiliar names of the Indians. And sometimes, like us, when we heard the cedars whisper it seem to be also a sign of happiness. So that's the Griffin family story about whispering cedars."

Bert sat in silence for several minutes, thinking of what Rose Anna had said. "If I had not heard myself, I might say that it was all just made up, but I did hear," he admitted, smiling at his wife. "This is something special. I wonder if in future years, descendants of the Griffin family will hear the cedars whisper?"

The cedars near the old home place would remain silent for many years. Bert and Rose Anna lived a long happy life, and were buried alongside family members on the hillside beside the grove of cedars. Some say when a gentle wind blows, they can still hear the names of Bert and Rose Anna softly floating in the wind.

Chapter 39
A Dam

Roda Lee, one of the daughters of Bert and Rose Anna, and her husband Henry, moved on down the river, making their home in a settlement known as Old Suzannah. Suzannah was a happy place, near the banks of a little creek that flowed with sparkling blue water. The people who lived there were good, hard-working, Christian folks who attended either the Baptist or the little Methodist Church every Sunday. The fertile soil produced good crops. The nearby river teemed with fish, and the hardwood forest abounded with wildlife. The little general country store provided everything the residents needed. There was a blacksmith shop and even a place where a man could go buy himself a drink. A school was built, and the children go all the way to sixth grade. The new century came, and with-it new ideas and progress as it was called.

On a cool, crisp day in October of 1921, Henry walked a short distance down the dirt road to the little store. Roda had just told him she wanted a new room added to the house, and he needed some nails.

"Come on in Henry, have a seat. There's some news going round you might be interested in," Jack the store owner said in greeting as other customers came into the store.

"What's going on, Jack?" Henry asked, grabbing a pickle out of a big jar on the counter.

"Well, there's some talk about a dam being built on the river," Jack informed.

"A dam!" One of the customers exclaimed, "why in the world would anybody want to build a dam?"

"So, we can have us some lights like them folks in the big cities do," another man added.

"Where they planning to put this dam?' Henry asked, frowning.

"Not sure, think they are still looking for the best place where the river is not so wide. Could be down at Cherokee

Bluffs," Jack answered.

"That means this land around here would be under water," Henry said, pausing, "Including ours here in Old Suzannah." Silence filled the room, each man realizing what Henry had said was true.

For the next few years, life at Old Suzannah continued on in a happy slow pace. Babies were born, old folks died, and life was good. Occasionally, word was heard about the dam, but so far it was just talk. Then one day, two men rode into town in a fancy Model T, their crisp white shirts soiled from the dust. The men went from door to door delivering their message to the shocked residents.

"We are with the Alabama Power Company," they announced. "The purpose of our visit is to purchase your property. A dam will be under construction, and when the structure is completed, your land will be under water."

Some families chose to take the offer, packing their belongings and leaving, buying land down river below the dam. Some moving as far as the old settlement of Reeltown and even farther. Others refused, watching as timber was cut, houses demolished, and the churches removed. The Old Suzannah folks and other communities along the river were filled with sadness, and sorrow when the dead were removed from their resting place to be reinterred far from their home.

Henry and Roda Lee would leave, living the remainder of their lives far from the old home place. One of their sons would stay, the water inching closer and closer each day, stopping just short of his home. Many times, Henry and Roda Lee would return to visit, standing on the bank of the vast body of water that had changed the lives of so many. They heard the cedars whisper as they swayed gently in the wind. Roda Lee was reminded of the stories her mother Rose Anna "Duck" Griffin Williams, had told of the Griffin family and of how they had lived and died, and they too had heard the timeless moan of the whispering cedars.

The End

Epilogue

My husband and I had driven for nearly an hour along the narrow country road that parallels the huge body of water known as the Tallapoosa River and Lake Martin. I was beginning to think the directions I had gotten from the Internet site were incorrect. Then after turning onto Williams Road, an even smaller road, going up one hill, and then another, and rounding one more curve, there it was ... the Williams Cemetery. Two large cedar trees gnarled with age standing guard over two headstones and eleven wooden crosses.

Stepping from the car into the warm summer sunshine, an immediate feeling of stepping back in time enveloped us. A little dog came running from a nearby house to meet us with a friendly greeting. I stood and read and read again the inscriptions on the old headstones. On the marker of a Confederate Soldier the name:

Egbert Williams
Company B 1st AL
State Troops CSA

And a simple square headstone placed beside the marker with the inscription:

Rose Anna Williams
Born April 2, 1846

The final resting place and gravesite of the people I had been searching for a long time. You may have guessed by now that I have a connection with these people. Rose Anna and Bert were my great- great grandparents.

Mesmerized, I gazed at the headstones, and then at the little crosses. Who was buried there? Was it family members, some children of Rose and Bert? Maybe her parents, John and Mary Griffin? So many unanswered questions, and I will probably never know the answer.

I realized that it was time to go. I looked at the grave site one final time, and then walked by the cedars. I experienced a strange feeling, and, in my head, a voice seemed to say, "You will be back. You have a story to write about me." I have always felt a connection with my great-great grandmother who had lived so long ago.

That has been several years, but I remember that strange feeling very well. Over time my husband and I, along with my mother, who has since passed away and my sister have returned to the gravesite. On one of the trips, I asked my husband to dig up a small cedar sprout that grew near the old tree. I told him I needed to take part of this past home with me. The cedar now is several feet tall, and still growing. Looking one day at the cedar we planted in our yard, I again heard that voice, "Write the story of your family." This inspired me to write about the Griffin family beginning seven or eight generations ago, around 1750. Most of these people actually lived and experienced the timely events of our country. Using family genealogy, documented names, dates and places were used. Of course, much is fiction, and reflects my family as I would have liked for them to have lived.

Could it be that the "Whispering Cedars" really did speak to me? We will never know, but the story of my family has been written, and I feel that all of it could have happened just this way.

Acknowledgments

Griffin Family Genealogy

The Cherokee People, Thomas E. Mails

Battle of Cowpens, The History Channel

Photographs

Williams Cemetery, Road Signs, Williams Home Place, Debra Hughey with Angie Moody and Sue Graben and the Author Standing at the Cedar at her home Fred Randall Hughey

Griffin Family Photograph

Williams/Curry Photograph

Patterson Log Cabin/Talisi Historical Preservation Society

Martin Dam, Alabama Power Company

Front Cover Photograph
Williams Cemetery, Dadeville, Alabama

Back Cover Photograph
The Author Debra Hughey Standing next to Transplanted Williams Cemetery Cedar at Her Home

Editing

Thanks to my friend, Pastor Rick Dorley for editing assistance and to Fred Randall Hughey, my wonderful husband. Thank you for your help, patience and love.

(Bottom Row) Griffin Sisters, Except Lady in the Center who is a Sister-In-Law. Rose Anna Griffin Williams is Likely One of These Women.

Family of Roda Lee Williams Curry, Rose Anna Griffin Williams' Daughter and Grand Children. Youngest Little Girl in White Dress is Julia Curry Wynn, the Author's Grandmother.

Williams Drive Leads to the Old Williams Cemetery, Home Site and Cemetery.

Road Named for the Old Settlement of Old Susanna.

Confederate Soldier Headstone of Egbert Williams and Rose Anna Griffin Williams Grave Markers at Williams Cemetery.

Likely the Site of the Old Williams Home Place,

Grave Marker of Rosanna (Rose Anna) Griffin Williams, the Author's Great, Great Grandmother at Williams Cemetery.

Author Debra Hughey (Center) and Distant Cousins, Angie Moody (Left) and Sue Graben (Right). The Williams Cemetery is Located in Mrs. Moody' Front Yard.

Construction of Martin Dam Circa 1928.

Martin Dam Today. The Lake Waters Completely Covered the Settlement of Old Susanna.

The Patterson Log Cabin in Tallassee, Alabama is an Example of an Early Pioneer's Dog Trot Cabin Similar to the Dwelling of the Griffin Family.

www.ingramcontent.com/pod-product-compliance
Lightning Source LLC
Chambersburg PA
CBHW070104080526
44586CB00013B/1179